Surviving My Husband's Stroke

A Wife's Emotional Journey as Caregiver for Her Post-stroke Husband

by Denise Hoover

The events and conversations in this book have been expressed to the best of the author's ability. Any resemblance to actual persons, living or dead, events, or locales is entirely coincidental.

www.denisehoover.com

Published by Midlife Choices LLC

ISBN 979-8-218-69285-8

Dearest Jeff,

In a single moment, life as we knew it changed forever. Yet through every challenge, every setback, and every small victory, my love for you has remained constant. Your courage in recovery inspired me to share our story, and your unwavering support gave me the strength to write it.

You are, and always will be, my everything.

I love you – heart, mind, and soul.

Denise

Our last selfie before the stroke.

Table of Contents

Introduction

*Promise me you'll always remember: You're
braver than you believe, and stronger than you
seem, and smarter than you think.*

Christopher Robin, Winnie the Pooh

The vital signs monitor glowed with green, crooked lines
and a blinking heart as I focused on my husband, lying in a
hospital bed—unaware of who he was or what was happening to
him. Our entire relationship flashed before my eyes. I didn't

know if we would have more time together or if our shared memories would end in that hospital room.

All my faith and hope rested in the hands of the doctors and nurses at our small-town hospital. I impatiently waited to see whether Jeff would live or die.

He lived.

But surviving the stroke was only the beginning. What followed was a journey neither of us was prepared for, transforming our lives in ways I never imagined.

The man I had built a life with now had to relearn the most basic tasks—from brushing his teeth to finding his way around our own home. Words that once flowed easily from his lips now struggled to escape his mouth. We worked tirelessly on identifying objects and pronouncing words. It felt like teaching a toddler about the world—every item unfamiliar, every word a challenge to master.

I was exhausted for months, constantly doubting whether I could survive this new role. I wasn't just his wife anymore—I was his caregiver.

Our carefully balanced marriage changed in an instant. Where we once had clearly defined roles, suddenly everything fell to me. Bills, home repairs, paperwork, decisions—I had to take it all on. My identity as Jeff's partner shifted into something I never expected: teacher, nurse, lifeline.

And as he struggled to relearn his world, I watched the man I loved fight to find himself again.

It was heartbreaking to witness—and at the same time, I was trying to figure out who I was in this new version of our life.

It tested every part of our relationship. We had always shared a deep, respectful love, and I took pride in being Jeff's wife. But nothing prepared me for the emotional weight of caregiving. I had a choice to make: wallow in self-pity or summon strength I didn't know I had.

I chose strength.

People often told me I was strong, but I had to start believing it myself. No matter how dark it got, I had to keep showing up—for Jeff and for me. My once-confident, strong-willed husband now looked to me for reassurance, for answers, for hope. Love meant being there even when I wanted to fall apart.

While this story includes Jeff's recovery, it's mostly about what it means to be a caregiver wife. It's about the moments when I didn't think I could take one more change, one more loss, one more reminder that life would never go back to the way it was.

It's about how Jeff changed.

It's about how I changed.

And it's about how we changed—together.

Some days felt unbearable. Others brought unexpected joy in the smallest victories. What follows is a memoir of that first year: the chaos, the heartbreak, the humor, the love, and the growth.

This memoir is about my journey through my husband's stroke recovery. You'll read about the hospital stay, the day we came home, the hard conversations, and the quiet moments in between—and what I did to survive it all.

At first, I thought I was writing this book for myself—as a form of therapy. But somewhere along the way, I realized that if I felt this alone, other women must be feeling it too.

Ultimately, I wrote this book for women like me—wives who suddenly find themselves navigating hospital corridors, managing medications, deciphering insurance, and carrying a weight they never asked for. One day you're doing ordinary things around the house. The next, you're managing your husband's rehabilitation schedule and wondering if your marriage will ever feel normal again.

When your world changes overnight, it helps to know someone else has been through it too.

This isn't a medical guide or a how-to manual. It's the story of one wife's journey through her husband's stroke recovery and ultimately her own recovery, offered as a companion to those walking a similar path.

If you're feeling overwhelmed—by fear, guilt, confusion, even resentment—you are not alone. The man you love may seem like a stranger right now. But somewhere inside, he's still there. And your love for who he was will help you support who he is becoming.

By sharing our first year of recovery, I hope to offer more than understanding. I hope to offer you permission—to grieve, to feel, to rest, and to grow.

You're not just part of someone else's recovery—you're on your own journey to survive.

Chapter 1
Tick, Tick, Tick

You never know how strong you are until being strong
is your only choice.

Bob Marley

"We're life-flighting your husband to Cleveland."
Wait. What?
My heart stopped. Life flight? That was for critical cases, for life-and-death situations. This was *my Jeff* they were talking

about, my fifty-six-year-old husband who had been working in the yard just hours ago.

A smug-looking man in his forties swept into the room with an air of condescending authority that made my skin crawl. He leaned against the counter with his arms and ankles crossed, barely looking up as he casually told me my husband was in a life-or-death situation. This seemed wildly inappropriate, like he was commenting on the weather. *Did he introduce himself? Is he the doctor? No white coat? Wouldn't a doctor deliver this news with a little more compassion? Shouldn't he be holding my hand, assuring me that everything would be okay?*

He was talking. I saw his lips moving, but I was frozen in place. My mind was cluttered. *Cleveland? That's almost an hour away. And then I'm going to have to stop at home and pack a bag. I'm not driving back and forth to Cleveland every day. Who's gonna take care of the dog? I should stay at the hospital with Jeff. Should I start calling hotels? Should I use my debit or credit card? I don't make these decisions. Jeff does.*

What if Jeff dies on the way there? Alone.

Oh. My. God.

The severity of the situation slapped me across the face. *Snap out of it, Denise. This man is explaining how they are going to save Jeff's life.*

"...we're just waiting for the doctors at University Hospital to review his scans. Once they give the okay, we'll life-flight him to Cleveland for surgery."

University Hospital? Life Flight? Surgery?

Brain surgery. Fuck.

The doctor, with his dark, slicked-back-hair attitude, turned and was gone. No further explanation. No questions asked or answered.

Questions bounced through my mind like a ping-pong ball. I should have chased him down the hall and interrogated him, but again, I stood frozen. A small ripple of calmness washed over me as I learned that more doctors were joining in the effort to save Jeff's life. However, a series of troubling questions began to arise in my mind: *What if they refuse to do the surgery? What are my options then? Can they refuse to do the surgery? Are they just going to let him die?* Negative scenarios took shape as I stood by Jeff's bed, staring down at a diminished version of my husband, waiting for answers.

Time was moving excruciatingly slow. The generic black and white clock was taunting me with its second hand. Tick. Tick. Tick. Each second that went by was another second they were not doing anything to save Jeff. A life-flight nurse walked in wearing his full gear. I asked if the helicopter had arrived. They were still waiting. *What the fuck were they waiting for? Can't they see my husband is lying here dying right in front of me?*

3

Jeff was looking at me, but not seeing me. His gaze was distant as if trying to recall who I was. He didn't know his name, birth date, or the year. I'm not sure if he knew what was happening to him, but somewhere in there, he knew something was wrong. Terrified he would die in his sleep, he was vigorously slapping his face with both hands, muttering, "Stay awake. Stay awake." My strong, confident husband was facing death and fearing it.

I was fearing his death, too. My best friend and soulmate was on the precipice of leaving me forever. Sweat formed on my upper lip as my breathing increased, and my hands began to shake. My heart rhythmically thumped in my ears. Panic ushered me out of that prison-like room through a maze of hallways and out the Emergency Room doors.

The empty red helicopter pad stood out boldly in the middle of the parking lot. A wave of sadness struck me for all those who were rushed to the helicopter for what might have been their last flight. My heartache intensified thinking Jeff might be one of them. I scanned the perfect summer sky, wishing to see the whirling blades as it came down for a landing. No helicopter. *How many times has a life flight flown over our house on the way to Cleveland?* Maybe Jeff could see our house one last time as they flew over. *What the fuck was taking so long?*

Back in the room, the man who was apparently the doctor, told me the doctors at University Hospital had decided the

4

surgery was too risky. Jeff's stroke was located too far back on the left side of his brain. It would be too complicated to do the surgery. He might not survive.

No brain surgery. The relief I felt was fleeting. *If they couldn't fix Jeff's brain with surgery, how would he survive this?*

They would attempt to stop Jeff's stroke by giving him a blood-thinning medication called TNK (Tenecteplase) to see if that would release the blood clots. It was explained to me that it was like Drano for Jeff's clogged arteries. The medicine would go into the veins and break up the clots. This had to be better than brain surgery.

A clipboard was handed to me with a stack of papers to sign. I scribbled my signature a few times without reading a word. If I didn't know the side effects of the medicine spelled out in those documents, I wouldn't obsess over them. I also never, ever asked Jeff's chance of survival. A living or dying percentage floating through my head would have been unbearable. For now, I was filled with eager anticipation that they were finally going to save my husband's life.

An hour ticked by without any medicine, as I impatiently paced next to Jeff's bed. Dread hung over me as each minute brought him closer to death.

What the fuck was taking so long? We had been waiting for almost three hours for something to be done to help Jeff. The medicine was supposed to be administered within three hours of his symptoms, or maybe it's four hours? Isn't that what I heard somewhere? *Why is there no sense of urgency?*

This rinky-dink, small-town hospital was going to let my husband die.

As I headed towards the door to seek answers, the nurse appeared. The miracle drug was clenched in her fist, by her side. I held my breath, watching her insert the TNK into Jeff's intravenous line (IV).

Tick, tick, tick. Moments in the Emergency Room (ER) last forever. You wait. And you think. And you wait. And you create the worst-case scenarios in your mind. *This has to work. It has to. Because if Jeff dies today, I don't know if I could survive losing him.*

A half-hour passed.

Jeff's eyes were gradually coming back into focus with a warmer, less confused look. The nurse charted his vitals. They were improving. He was becoming more alert. A glimpse of the old Jeff made me tear up. The medicine was working. This was my first glimmer of hope since we walked through the ER doors.

Exhale. *He's going to be okay. He's going to live. He's coming back to me.*

After spending over four hours in the local hospital, Jeff was transported to a hospital in the next county over. They had a trauma unit that would be better equipped to take care of him.

The Emergency Medical Team (EMTs) arrived rather quickly after he received the TNK.

Bending down to Jeff's forehead, I gave him a lingering kiss, "I love you. I'll be there as quick as I can."

Then, I turned toward the two scraggly-looking twenty-somethings and said in a stern voice, "Take good care of him. He's precious cargo."

The twenty-five-minute drive felt more manageable than the long haul to Cleveland, but I had to stop at home first to let the dog out, grab a sweater, and pick up a book. Then I thought about what else I might need at the hospital: Jeff's Power of Attorney and Living Will. I always hoped those were documents we'd never actually have to use. Tears streamed down my face as I searched through our filing cabinet, then the box where we kept important papers. Nothing. Panic rose as I remembered that Jeff kept some documents in his desk. I yanked open the drawer and finally found them. For a few moments, I just stared at them, wishing they weren't necessary, but knowing I had to be prepared. I shoved them into my purse and rushed out the door.

The drive was a blur. I'm not sure if I followed any kind of traffic laws. Music softly played in the background as I contemplated the events of our morning.

The uncertainty of Jeff's future was tearing me up inside. My overthinking demeanor ran on loop the whole way there:

Okay. Okay. Okay. The medicine is working. That's a good thing.

But what if it stops working?

Will they give him more?

Is there still a chance he could die? Oh my god. What if he dies?

What if I'm alone?

If he lives, what's he going to be like?

> *Can he recover fully from this?*

How long will recovery take?

Please don't let him die before I get there.

Please don't let him die before I get there.

Anticipating a panic attack, I white-knuckled the steering wheel, reminding myself to breathe. I took the deepest inhale as I pulled into the hospital parking lot. *I'm coming, Jeff.*

At a fast pace, I made it through the hot asphalt parking lot, tripping up the sidewalk. The automatic doors gradually slid open with a rush of cold air. The harsh fluorescent lights overhead seemed to put a spotlight on the gravity of the situation. The hushed voices of staff and family members created a tense murmur that seemed to pulse through the pristine waiting room. I rushed over to the round circular desk anchored in the middle of the room.

I gripped the edge of the information desk, its cool surface grounding me as I fought to keep my voice steady, "They brought my husband here from another hospital. He's somewhere in the ICU."

"Name?" She inquired in a monotone manner as if she were calling out "Next" at the Department of Motor Vehicles (DMV).

"Uh. Hoover. Jeff Hoover. Well, Jeffrey Hoover."

She handed me a visitor sticker and said, "Bed 1A."

"Can you tell me how to get there? I don't know where the ICU is." *It's unfortunate that I had to ask. Can't she see how flustered I was?*

A persistent feeling of dread hung over me as I hurried through endless hallways to the Intensive Care Unit (ICU). *Please let him be alive. Please let him be alive.*

Exhaling deeply, I felt relief wash over me when I entered his room. Jeff was alert. His eyes were open. *He's alive.*

Jeff was sitting upright in the hospital bed. His eyes slightly sparkled with amusement when I entered the room. *He knows me.* As quickly as I caught a glimpse of the old Jeff, he vanished. The confused, blank stare returned, and I didn't exist anymore. The tension between fear and relief was taking a toll on my heart. I imagined it shattering into a thousand tiny pieces if Jeff did not survive this.

There were two nurses in the room tending to Jeff. One stood at her portable computer stand, typing information into his chart. The other nurse was adjusting the pillows behind Jeff's back. They both turned towards me when I entered the room.

I rapidly started spewing out questions with a quivering voice, "Have they found out more about his stroke? When does he get the medicine again? What other tests are they going to run?" I stopped to catch my breath.

The older of the two nurses came over and gently whispered, "Sit down, honey. He's going to be okay." She paused, "And it's okay to cry."

Without warning, my body began heaving. Through uncontrollable crying, I gasped from deep within my soul, "I don't want this to be the end of our love story." After hours of being strong, my heart finally spoke its truth.

Rubbing my back, the nurse assured me, "We are doing everything we can for him. He's in good hands. He's making great progress with just getting the medicine not that long ago." Gratitude filled me as I finally received compassion from someone.

As the nurse's words faded, I noticed something wrong—Jeff hadn't reacted to my emotional outburst at all. This wasn't the Jeff I knew. My husband had always been my rock, reaching for my hand before I even knew I needed it. Now he just stared at me, his eyes vacant, offering nothing.

The thought hit me like a gut punch: *If he makes it through this, will he ever really come back to me?*

Before the stroke, Jeff was the one I leaned on. Jeff navigated our life's challenges with unwavering strength. He made decisions with this quiet confidence I'd always envied but relied on completely. While I deliberated and analyzed, he just knew which direction to take. We balanced each other perfectly that way.

But now? He looked at me with empty curiosity, like I was a stranger speaking a language he couldn't quite place. No comfort. No reassurance. Just... absence.

Everything was flipping upside down. The finances, our future plans, the big life decisions he'd always handled would now fall on me. Each responsibility felt like another weight being added to my shoulders, already heavy with grief for the man lying in front of me.

Maybe I'd absorbed more from watching him all these years than I realized. But the thought of permanently becoming the decision-maker, the rock, the compass—it terrified me. What would we become if our dance of give and take turned into just me, stumbling forward alone, dragging both of us toward whatever came next?

As I watched Jeff's confused expression, I wondered how our relationship would evolve. Could I summon the strength to handle all the decision-making if he remained unable to participate? The thought of permanently losing our previous dynamic – the easy flow of our shared life – felt unbearable.

But this was not the time for such thoughts. I closed my eyes, took a deep breath, and composed myself—*worries for another day.*

As I sat in the uncomfortable hospital chair, clutching Jeff's hand as he slept, my thoughts drifted off to what happened that morning.

Chapter 2
Something's Wrong

The disease might hide the person underneath, but there's still a person in there who needs your love and attention.

Jamie Calandriello

It was a random Sunday in June, the kind of morning where the humidity already hinted at the scorching day ahead. Jeff was out back moving stone pavers to make a little pad for my hose reel. I was on the elliptical inside. It was an average Sunday morning like so many we had before. Our plans involved attending a softball game, then heading to a friend's house for a cookout—just another summer weekend.

When I finished my morning exercises, I went to tell Jeff I was jumping in the shower. He was leaning on the deck railing with one hand and had a glass of water in the other, his t-shirt covered in dirt and sweat. His eyes were unfocused, almost zombie-like.

He staggered over to a chair and unsteadily sat down.

"Are you ok?" I asked with confusion. I had never seen Jeff's eyes look so blank.

He stared at me, unsteadily made his way up to the deck, and sat in another chair. The second time I asked if he was alright, a sentence of jumbled words came out of his mouth. He was speaking actual words, but he wasn't making sense.

Suddenly, a Facebook post I'd read the week before flashed through my mind. It was about a woman who died of a stroke because no one recognized the early warning signs. The post had outlined the symptoms—droopy face, slurred speech—and suggested simple tests you could do if you suspected someone was having a stroke. That PSA might have just saved my husband's life.

Bending near him, I nervously asked, "Can you smile for me?" He could barely raise the corners of his mouth.

"Can you do this with your arms?" I lifted my arms at a parallel height, palms down. Jeff looked down at his arms as if willing them to move, but they remained on the chair.

"We're going to the hospital. Something is wrong with you."

He shook his head defiantly, uttering another incoherent sentence.

After the second time, he refused, I firmly shouted, "I am fucking taking you to the hospital. Now go into the house and change your clothes." *Why did I feel he needed to change out of his dirty clothes to go to the hospital?*

Jeff entered the house, rubbing his head. He slowly shuffled down the hall to our room.

I stood paralyzed in the living room, but while fear held my body still, my mind automatically shifted into crisis mode, frantically cycling through questions about what to do next.

Should I call 911? *No, we live in a small town with a volunteer fire department. It would take too long for them to get here, evaluate him, and take him to the hospital.*

Should I take him to the hospital? *Yes, probably. There's definitely something wrong.*

Should I wait a little bit and see if it gets better? *No, Denise, this is fucking serious.*

Who can I call for help? Who do I know in the medical field? *I have a friend who's like a brother to me, and he's a nurse. He'll know if I should take Jeff to the hospital. I'll call him.*

I grabbed my phone, looked him up, and hit the green button. One ring, two rings, three rings, voicemail. I hung up. *Shit, I forgot he's working today.* I didn't leave a message.

Jeff walked into the living room, still in the same dirt-stained clothes he had on while moving the pavers. The disoriented, panicked look in his eyes was haunting.

"Why didn't you change your clothes?" *Again, did he need to look presentable at the hospital?*

When he didn't respond, I took him by the arm, guided him to the bedroom, and helped him change his clothes. We were definitely heading to the hospital.

The drive to the hospital was surreal. Jeff sat silently in the passenger seat, occasionally rubbing his head, while I squeezed the steering wheel in a vice-like hold, barely able to loosen my grip. Every red light felt like an eternity. I kept glancing over at him, trying to gauge if he was getting worse, wondering if I should have called that ambulance after all.

The emergency room doors slid open to reveal a surprisingly quiet waiting area. Jeff staggered beside me, his movements uncertain. As we approached the desk, I told him to sit in the first chair I saw. The true severity of the situation didn't sink in until we spoke to the person behind the glass.

"Something's wrong with my husband. He's not making sense. And his eyes are glazed over."

After taking his information, the desk attendant immediately came around from behind the glass. She asked Jeff his name, birth date, and what year it was. He couldn't answer her. *Oh fuck. This is serious.*

She asked him if he could walk. I answered for him, "Yes, he's not having any trouble physically." Swiftly, she took him back to a room. And my only thought was, *Thank God we didn't have to sit in the waiting room for hours.*

I knew he must be having a stroke, but I was rationalizing that it couldn't be that serious. After all, he wasn't paralyzed on one side of his body, and his face wasn't drooping. If he wasn't showing these symptoms, I thought, maybe they could give him some medicine and we'd be back to our ordinary Sunday. The symptoms concerning me were his jumbled speech and lack of memory. *But that could be fixed with medicine, and we'd be on our way. Right?*

As I helped Jeff into his hospital gown, I clung to the desperate hope that this was just a minor medical issue. At fifty-something, it seemed too soon to be helping my husband dress. In our twenty-seven years together, I never imagined becoming Jeff's caregiver. Our story was supposed to be simpler: growing old side by side, peacefully drifting off together one night. That's the perfect ending I have always imagined. Unfortunately, real life is not like the love story ending in the movies. In real life, we get shitty things thrown at us all the time. We were living one of those real-life shitty moments right now, in the ER, dealing with something neither one of us could have anticipated. All we could do was wait for answers, for tests, for someone to tell us what was wrong with Jeff. And I was never good at waiting.

I despise being in the Emergency Room. It's a lot of waiting and waiting and waiting. I have no patience for that. I understand, logically, that proper procedures must be followed, and others may have more urgent needs. But when it's *my husband* in the ER, I need regular communication. Being left for hours without updates only feeds my anxiety. With Jeff's condition already sending my mind racing, the silence gave too much space for worst-case scenarios to take root. Some information, any information, would help calm my spiraling thoughts. Instead of imagining the worst, I needed to focus on our immediate situation.

The weight of notifying family and friends pressed against my chest, but I couldn't face the thought of repeatedly explaining Jeff's condition. Each retelling would force me to confront our new reality, and I knew I would break down. I needed a different approach.

I devised a careful strategy. For my family, I chose one sister as the messenger, asking her to inform the others while making it clear: no group messages, no phone calls. I needed space to process without constant interruptions. I applied the same method with Jeff's family, selecting a single point person to spread the word under the same conditions.

Among our friends, I thought of two who would understand the delicate balance between support and space. Their steadiness would become crucial in the days ahead. As for social media, that announcement could wait until I had more concrete information and felt better equipped to handle the inevitable flood of responses.

In that moment, self-preservation trumped people-pleasing. I needed to conserve every ounce of emotional energy for what lay ahead. Speaking the words aloud—"Jeff had a stroke"— would make this nightmare real, and I wasn't ready for that yet. My focus needed to stay on my husband.

Standing in his hospital room now, watching nurses connect him to various machines, the morning's events felt like a distant dream. Just hours ago, we'd been living a normal Sunday. Now here I was, standing by Jeff's hospital bed, wondering if he was going to survive.

I took a deep breath, steadying myself against what was coming. The smug doctor's words still rang in my ears: "We're life-flighting your husband to Cleveland." Those words had marked the beginning of this nightmare, and now, as I stood vigil by Jeff's bedside in the ICU, I realized they were just a gateway to a much longer journey.

Our love story wasn't ending, but it was taking a turn I never expected. As I gripped Jeff's hand, I knew everything would be different from this moment on. I was no longer just a wife; I was a caregiver and an advocate for my husband's life. The weight of this new reality settled on my shoulders as I prepared myself for the fight ahead.

Chapter 3
Those First Few Days

No matter what happens, or how bad it seems today,
life does go on, and it will be better tomorrow.

Maya Angelou

Jeff spent two nights in the ICU and one night in a regular hospital room. During visiting hours, I made his room my temporary home, setting up camp at the foot of his bed. Jeff's tray table and a spare chair held my survival kit: snacks, Kindle, laptop, phone, journal, and various chargers. The only natural light filtered through the window at the head of his bed, while the steady beep of the heart monitor became my constant companion, punctuated by the occasional whispers of the nurses at their station. The sharp smell of disinfectant hung in the air, a constant reminder of where we were. As I shifted in the rigid pleather chair, my hand absently traced the cool metal of the bed rail, I searched for ways to distract myself.

I tried watching Suits, but it didn't hold my attention. My business book seemed trivial now. Royal Match kept me occupied until I ran out of lives. Eventually, I fell back on my usual stress coping mechanisms: popcorn, M&Ms, Doritos, chocolate, too many chai lattes, and cigarettes. Salt, sugar, and nicotine—the familiar comforts I turned to when everything else felt out of control.

The cigarettes became both my escape and my burden at the hospital. They gave me an excuse to leave the room and momentarily calm my nerves, but each break came with growing guilt. My husband had just had a stroke, and here I was, still clinging to this unhealthy habit. I needed to quit, but at this moment, I needed my cigarettes more.

Standing outside, each inhale brought a mix of relief and self-loathing. The familiar rush of nicotine steadied my nerves, providing a momentary escape from the sterile hospital environment and the weight of our new reality. Yet with each exhale, guilt crept in. Here I was, indulging in a habit that could lead me down the same path as Jeff. The irony wasn't lost on me.

I contemplated quitting right then and there, imagining how proud Jeff would be if I could kick the habit while he fought for his recovery. But the thought of facing this ordeal without my crutch terrified me. How could I be strong for Jeff if I were battling my own demons?

I told myself that quitting now would only add to the overwhelming stress of our situation. I needed my crutch, at least until he recovered. It was a bargain I made with myself—a promise to change once the storm had passed. But beneath that promise lurked a troubling doubt. If I wasn't strong enough to quit, how could I possibly be strong enough to care for Jeff the way he needed? Was I postponing my decision for the right reasons, or was I just proving to myself that I wasn't as strong as I needed to be?

As I put out the cigarette and headed back inside, I made a silent vow to quit someday. For now, these brief escapes were keeping me sane, allowing me to face whatever came next. It wasn't ideal, but it was the best I could do in this moment of crisis.

One time, after having a smoke, I walked into Jeff's room, and he was gone. I ran over to the nurse's station and said, "Where did they take my husband?" In those few seconds, my mind jumped to the worst conclusions. I was told he had been taken for an MRA, a type of MRI that examines blood vessels, specifically the arteries in his head. But those moments of terror stayed with me. What if he had another AFib episode, or worse, while I was outside smoking? The guilt was suffocating, yet I still couldn't quit—not yet. These breaks were keeping me functional, allowing me to face whatever came next.

I was only gone for ten minutes. Am I going to get panicky every time I can't find Jeff? I'm definitely going to quit smoking. I wouldn't forgive myself if something happened to him while I was out having a cigarette. But during those days in the hospital, it was a much-needed distraction.

Journaling proved to be the worst distraction of all. While other activities were meant to keep my mind from unthinkable thoughts, writing unleashed every fear I'd been trying to suppress. My thoughts spilled onto the page, then ricocheted back into my head with renewed intensity.

Why did this happen to us? The ten-year obligation of taking care of his parents ended two months ago when his mom passed away. We'd retired early, started traveling, and were enjoying our freedom. *Is it ever going to be that way again?*

Why did this happen to Jeff? Overall, he's a healthy fifty-six-year-old man with no medical history. *Will he fully recover from this? Will he ever be normal again? What if he has another stroke? What if he dies?*

Why did this happen to me? Could I handle being his caregiver? Was I strong enough? How long would this last? How would this change me? What if I become a widow?

It was an endless cycle of what-ifs. My mind was repeatedly tormented with similar questions. *What will our life be like now? What if he never recovers? How am I going to handle this? What if he doesn't make it?* The questions compounded, none offering answers or comfort. I tossed my journal into my tote, hoping to avoid the constant thoughts of Jeff's condition.

But the moment I was alone at home that first night, the silence was unbearable. Every fear and doubt I had pushed aside during the day came rushing back, making sleep impossible. Remembering I still needed to notify friends and family through social media, I grabbed paper and pen, struggling for an hour to find words to describe my husband almost dying. Even then, I couldn't bring myself to hit "Submit" until morning.

Here's the actual post:

It's amazing to me how things can change in an instant. We took this picture Saturday night at a local festival. (see pic on dedication page) We had a great time talking to people I went to high school with and others who Jeff worked with.

Sunday morning started with me doing things in the house and Jeff working outside to move some stone pavers to make room for the hot tub we bought last week. When I went out to talk to him, he wasn't making sense. His words were jumbled, and I couldn't understand him. I knew this was one of the symptoms of a stroke. I took him to the hospital immediately.

They verified that Jeff was having a stroke and wanted to life flight him to University in Cleveland, but once the doctors at University read his scans, they said the location of the blood clot was too risky for surgery. They began treating him with an anticoagulant to break up the clot.

He was then transferred to University Hospital in Claridon (Geauga County), where they are better equipped to handle this situation.

Because the clot was on the left side of his brain, Jeff has aphasia. This means the stroke affected his speech and communication. It's so hard to watch him fight to get the right words out.

I'm devastated over this. I don't know what our future looks like now. He is my best friend, my soul mate, my life partner. I love him so much, this is just breaking my heart.

Spoke with his nurse around 4 AM. He is in stable condition and will be having an MRI this morning around 8 AM. He is making slight improvements in his speech.

I'm not a religious person, but I do believe in the power of prayer. So say a little prayer for Jeff today.

I'll try to keep adding updates when I get a chance.

It was challenging to find a balance between being too emotional and providing the details of what happened. As I sat alone writing it, I was having an emotional breakdown. *What the fuck just happened to our lives? This is going to change everything. Jeff will never be the same person he was before his stroke, and neither will I. The person he was is gone. I already miss him.* A sense of loneliness washed over me as I hugged his t-shirt, pulled from the laundry basket, and cried myself to sleep.

Panic jolted me awake at 4 AM. *What if he hadn't made it through the night? Surely, they would have called me. Why didn't I stay at the hospital with him?* The nurses told me visiting hours were over at 9:00, so I just left. I was completely overtaken by exhaustion. I accepted it as fact that I had to leave. I didn't even put up a fight. I may have left my husband to die alone in the hospital. *How guilty would I have felt if he had died alone?*

Wondering if it was too early to call the hospital, I typed in the number. I had to know Jeff was still alive and didn't have any complications throughout the night. Speaking to the ICU nurse, a wave of reassurance swept through me. Jeff was alive and did well throughout the night. The doctor would be doing his rounds at 8:30 if I wanted to talk to him. We hadn't seen a doctor that first day, but I would definitely be there this morning to talk to one.

On the way to the hospital, Bon Jovi's "Never Say Goodbye" came on the radio. The tears started flowing. My husband was alive, but thoughts of him never being normal again flooded me with emotion. Through blurred vision, I wondered what our "new normal" would look like. Would I have to assist him with everyday tasks for the rest of my life? What kind of future could we have now that my husband has brain damage? Was this the end of our happily ever after?

For twenty-seven years, we had written our own love story, each being a main character. Jeff was the Prince Charming who swept me off my feet, and I was his princess. I couldn't help but wonder if I would get my soulmate back. Our love for one another was unlike any other bond I had felt in my life. *Would we still be able to hold onto those immense feelings we had for each other? Or was this the beginning of the deterioration of our relationship?*

These thoughts harassed me on the drive to the hospital. I was preoccupied with how Jeff's stroke would affect me and our relationship. Nevertheless, Jeff was the one whose brain had been damaged. The damage I suffered was to my heart, and that could heal if he were able to recover from this. I would have to get answers from the doctors about how severely the stroke affected him and what his recovery would look like.

Chapter 4
How Bad is He?

You are not your illness. You have an individual story
to tell. You have a name, a history, a personality.
Staying yourself is part of the battle.

Julian Seifter

The initial reports from the doctors were encouraging. Jeff was doing well. The arteries in his brain were clear of clots, and with time and therapy, he should recover. They suggested it would take three to six months for a full recovery. But as I watched my husband struggle in the hospital, I questioned their optimistic prognosis.

Immediately after his stroke, Jeff had apraxia—difficulty with movements despite understanding what he was being asked to do and knowing how to do it. When told to touch his right knee, he'd touch his shin. Asked to blow air out of his mouth, he'd just puff up his cheeks. After each incorrect action, he'd vigorously nod and ask, "Yeah? Yeah? Yeah?" seeking approval, unaware of his mistakes. His brain told him he was following directions correctly, but the apraxia prevented him from doing so.

Even simple, everyday tasks were affected. Eating with utensils became his first relearning challenge. I taught him how to hold a fork and bring a cup to his mouth. Watching Jeff struggle with these basic tasks crushed my spirit. *Am I going to have to teach him how to do everything when we get home?* I desperately hoped this wouldn't be our future. The thought of caring for someone who struggled to feed himself terrified the hell out of me.

Though this may sound selfish to some, this was my initial reaction following the stroke. *My husband, whom I love with all my heart and soul, needs me now, and I'm unsure if I can handle it.* I know some people find fulfillment in caring for loved ones, but I'm not one of them. Despite feeling this way, I continued to aid him throughout his hospital stay, attempting to push aside my apprehension. Jeff needed me.

And maybe that's what was bothering me the most... I needed him. Jeff was the one who always took care of me. *Who is going to take care of me now?* I set aside this thought for another time. It was more important to focus my energy towards getting him through his hospital stay and, in a position, to go home.

At the hospital, Jeff was introduced to physical, occupational, and speech therapy. He relearned how to eat and drink, go to the bathroom, change his clothes, and methods of pronouncing words. He was making minor improvements. I paid close attention to everything the nurses and therapists did, hoping to learn as much as possible before taking Jeff home. If I could help with his recovery, maybe he would improve faster. Perhaps, with my assistance, he could make a full recovery.

During his hospital stay, my most important task was to help Jeff with hygiene. Brushing his teeth became an exercise in breaking down a simple task into its most basic components. I had to guide Jeff through each step, from identifying the toothbrush and toothpaste to the actual brushing motion.

"This is toothpaste," I'd begin, holding up the tube. "And this is your toothbrush."

Slowly, I'd demonstrate how to unscrew the cap, apply the paste to the brush, and bring it to his mouth. Each movement required detailed instructions and often a physical demonstration.

"Now, move the brush side-to-side and up-and-down in your mouth," I'd explain, mimicking the motion.

After brushing, I'd guide him through rinsing and spitting into a basin. The entire process, once an unconscious routine, now took painstaking effort and concentration.

It was odd that once he practiced these simple tasks a few times, he could do them independently without any problem. But initially, every step had to be taught as if it were a completely new skill.

While the apraxia faded quickly in the hospital, the aphasia would take longer to overcome. Jeff was diagnosed with mild receptive aphasia and moderate expressive aphasia—damage to the part of his brain affecting language. Receptive aphasia made it difficult to understand what others were saying. Expressive aphasia meant he knew what he wanted to say but couldn't get the words out. Both his speech and comprehension would need work in therapy. Yet surprisingly, Jeff could still write. When asked by his neurologist, he correctly wrote his name and address. It was during that assessment with the neurologist that I learned Jeff had suffered a major stroke.

No one had used the word "major" before this. Why did it take three days for someone to tell me this was a MAJOR stroke? The word hit me like a physical blow, forcing the air from my lungs. Major. It seemed to echo throughout the hospital room, each repetition carrying new weight, new implications.

I felt a surge of anger. *How could they have kept this from me for three days? Had they been sugarcoating Jeff's condition? What else weren't they telling me?* The anger quickly gave way to fear as the full impact of "major" sank in. Major meant serious. Major meant life-changing. Major meant our world as we knew it might never be the same again. I glanced at Jeff, peacefully unaware of this new label attached to his condition. Did he understand the seriousness of what had happened to him? Did I?

Questions raced through my mind, each one opening up new avenues of worry. *How "major" was major? What did this mean for Jeff's recovery? For our future?* The doctors' earlier optimism now seemed at odds with this new information. Could I trust their prognosis, or was this just the beginning of a much longer, more difficult journey?

I wanted to interrupt the neurologist to demand answers to all these questions swirling in my head. But I remained silent, nodding mechanically as she continued her explanation. I needed to hear everything before I could even begin to process this new reality.

The neurologist explained that Jeff's stroke was caused by his heart going into atrial fibrillation (AFib). Blood had pooled in his heart, forming clots that broke loose and traveled to his brain. The blood flow in four of his brain arteries had been restricted, causing the stroke.

She expressed disbelief at Jeff's lack of physical damage. Having seen similar cases, she couldn't comprehend how he'd avoided paralysis or even death. Major strokes like this usually left survivors with physical restrictions or paralysis. This case, she said, was one she'd remember for her entire career. Her words lingered in my mind, prompting questions about life, miracles, and alternative outcomes.

As I stood by Jeff's hospital bed, watching him struggle with the simplest tasks, the weight of our new reality settled over me. The word "major" echoed in my mind, a stark reminder of how close we had come to losing everything. Yet, amidst the fear and uncertainty, there was an undeniable miracle—Jeff had survived without physical paralysis, defying medical expectations. However, even as I clung to the relief of his survival, a new kind of fear took hold—one that had nothing to do with Jeff's condition and everything to do with my own ability to handle what lay ahead.

My doubts gnawed at me. *Could I be the caregiver Jeff needed? Was I strong enough to guide him through this long recovery?* The thought of teaching him all the basic skills he needed felt overwhelming. I wasn't sure if I could handle it, and the guilt of these thoughts only added to my burden.

34

But as I watched Jeff's determined efforts to relearn even the simplest movements, I felt a spark of resolve ignite within me. This wasn't just Jeff's battlefield, it was ours. His miracle of survival demanded something of both of us: courage in the face of an uncertain future.

I realized then that my journey of recovery lay ahead— learning to be a caregiver, to find strength I didn't know I possessed. As I helped Jeff navigate his new world, I had to navigate my fears and doubts. It wouldn't be easy, but Jeff's miraculous survival reminded me that sometimes, against all odds, we find the strength to persevere. With a deep breath, I steeled myself for the challenging road ahead, determined to face it together, one small victory at a time.

Chapter 5
Back to the Basics

You can rise up from anything. You can completely recreate yourself. Nothing is permanent. You are not stuck. You have choices. You can think new thoughts. You can learn something new. You can create new habits. All that matters is that you decide today and never look back.

Idil Ahmed

On the day Jeff was being released, I stood in the elementary education section of Walmart, wondering what would help in his recovery. This was what my life had come to — choosing elementary flashcards and workbooks for my husband. Would these even help? With barely any guidance online about helping stroke survivors recover, I would have to rely on my instincts and educational background to reteach Jeff the things that were once on autopilot.

Being home meant he would have to learn how to shower, shave, and put his contacts in. While he attempted these tasks independently, I would monitor his progress and provide guidance when needed. We started with basic hygiene items. *The shampoo is to wash your hair. The soap is to wash your body. This razor and shaving cream are used to shave your face.* These simple, daily routines that should have been easy became lessons I never would have imagined teaching my husband. My irritation grew every time I had to repeatedly show him how to do something. If assisting him with the simple tasks in life frustrated me, how would I handle the rest of his recovery?

Despite the severity of Jeff's stroke, the hospital sent us home without a roadmap. No instructions on what to watch for, no guidelines on how to care for a stroke survivor, no manual for what to do if things go wrong. They taught me specific tasks like helping him brush his teeth, but nobody prepared me for the bigger picture of being a caregiver to a stroke survivor. It felt like being pushed into the deep end without knowing how to swim. I would need to discover my own path forward to assist Jeff in his recovery.

Teaching had always been second nature to me, but I never imagined I'd be applying those skills to help my husband relearn the basics of daily life. As I stepped into this unexpected role, I found myself drawing on techniques typically used with young children, adapting them to Jeff's unique situation.

I became an elementary teacher of sorts, guiding Jeff to reacquaint himself with letters, numbers, everyday objects, and their spellings. The key, I realized, was repetition—a fundamental principle in early childhood education. Just as a child learns to recognize letters or colors through consistent exposure and practice, I believed Jeff's stroke-affected brain could benefit from a similar approach.

This realization led me to develop what I called the "box of everyday things." It was a simple yet effective tool, born out of necessity and intuition. By repeatedly showing Jeff common items, having him name and spell them, I hoped to reacquaint him with the loss of information caused by the stroke. It was a methodical process, but one that I believed could help Jeff reclaim the knowledge that was locked away in his healing brain.

The box contained items from our bedroom, office, bathroom, and kitchen. Jeff would write down the names of the objects and identify them verbally without looking at what he wrote. In the beginning, he couldn't identify a key or tell the difference between utensils. I would replace the items he got correct daily. The ones he got wrong would remain in the box. The spoon, knife, and fork remained in the box for a week. Once recognizing everyday items became easy for him, we moved on to more difficult things.

Next, I gave Jeff alphabet worksheets displaying a picture for each letter. He would write what each picture was underneath. Wrench and stool were two objects he could not identify or understand their purpose. After explaining these items to him, I had to put a wrench and stool in the living room for him to look at every day. Eventually, he learned how to name them and understand their use. It baffled me how he could identify certain things while being unable to recognize others.

Jeff also struggled with what day it was. He needed to learn the date and the days of the week. I put an 8″ x 9″ whiteboard on the refrigerator with "Today is..." written at the top. Every morning, he would write the day of the week, the month, the day, and the year. It took him three weeks to master this. We continued working on basic tasks while also incorporating more complex lessons for his recovery.

Along with these basics, we had to work on his comprehension. The receptive aphasia made it difficult for him to grasp ideas as he read. The speech therapist gave me short stories to read to Jeff, and he would answer questions about each story. We also worked on list building. I would give him prompts like "name five fruits or "name five pieces of furniture." These comprehension activities challenged him at first, but eventually became easier.

Jeff's struggle with speech proved to be one of the most challenging aspects of his recovery. His inability to articulate thoughts was not only frustrating for him but heartbreaking for me to witness. In an attempt to overcome this hurdle, Jeff developed a unique coping mechanism that I came to call "letter counting."

When Jeff found himself unable to speak a particular word, he would recite the alphabet aloud, touching each finger as if he were counting. It was as though he was searching through a mental filing cabinet, hoping to stumble upon the forgotten word. As he progressed through the letters, he would slow down when he approached the first letter of the word he was trying to say. Then, suddenly, upon reaching that letter, the word would burst forth from his mouth, often startling both of us with its abruptness.

This method, while effective, was a stark reminder of how much the stroke had altered his cognitive processes. Watching my once articulate husband reduced to sounding out the alphabet to find a single word was both fascinating and distressing. It was like watching his brain create a detour, forging new neural pathways out of necessity.

Jeff reciting the alphabet became a familiar sound in our home. Over time, I found myself silently cheering each time a word successfully emerged. It was a small victory, but in the world of stroke recovery, we learned to celebrate every step forward, no matter how small.

The speech therapist explained that this method was actually beneficial for his recovery, forcing his brain to make new connections and potentially speeding up his language recovery. Still, I couldn't help but long for the day when Jeff could speak freely again, without this alphabetical crutch.

When he wasn't using the alphabet to find his words, he would pause or stutter if the words didn't come to him. At first, when we were around people, I felt the need to finish Jeff's sentences or prompt him with the word he was trying to say. The speech therapist taught me that he needed to figure out the words himself—it helped him build those connections from brain to mouth. His friends had adapted to his new way of speaking, but I found it more frustrating.

The transformation in our communication was perhaps one of the most significant and heart-wrenching changes in our relationship. Where once we engaged in lively, free-flowing conversations that spanned a lot of topics, now our exchanges had become constrained and frustratingly basic.

Jeff had always been my confidant, the one person I could turn to with my thoughts, fears, and dreams. Our discussions would often drift from subject to subject, an assortment of ideas and shared experiences. Now, I had to consciously slow my speech, carefully choosing simple words and sticking to one subject at a time. It felt unnatural, as if I were suddenly speaking a foreign language in my own home.

The need to simplify my communication left me feeling isolated. Complex ideas or subtle emotions that I longed to share became trapped within me, unable to bridge the gap the stroke created between us. I caught myself censoring my thoughts, reducing complicated, layered thoughts to their most basic elements. It was like trying to put a puzzle together without the edge pieces.

This new reality was especially difficult given my tendency to ramble and jump between topics in conversation. I had to constantly check myself, reining in my natural way of speaking. It was mentally exhausting, and at times, I felt as if I were losing a part of myself in the process.

The loss of our previous back-and-forth conversations left a void in our relationship. Jeff had been the one person with whom I could fully be myself, sharing my beliefs and ideas without filters. Now, I found myself craving the kind of deep, rambling discussions we used to have. The inability to fully express myself to my life partner left me feeling oddly alone, even when we were together.

I grappled with feelings of guilt over these frustrations. After all, Jeff was the one struggling to communicate at all. Yet I couldn't shake the sense of loss – the loss of my conversational partner, my sounding board, the one who challenged and engaged me in every discussion. I longed for the day when we could once again lose ourselves in long, winding conversations, but for now, I had to adapt to this new, simplified form of communication, all while searching for new outlets for my more complex thoughts and feelings.

Friends and family regularly checked on me, showing concern and support. There was hesitation on my part to discuss the mental breakdown I was enduring. I internalized my feelings, not wanting to burden my support system. My personality was always to be positive and never show my anxiety or fears to anyone but Jeff. Now that my best friend was unavailable for conversations, I didn't know who to share my feelings and emotions with.

After two weeks of internalizing my tumultuous emotions, I reached my breaking point. The weight of unspoken fears and anxieties had become too heavy to bear alone. With trepidation, I turned to my sister, hoping she could be the person I could finally open up to.

As we sat together, I began unloading the dark thoughts that had been plaguing me in the quiet hours of the night. I confessed how I'd developed the habit of falling asleep on Jeff's chest, ear pressed to his heart, vigilantly listening to each beat.

"I'm terrified," I admitted, my voice barely above a whisper. "I'm scared of his heart stopping in the middle of the night. I'm hoping I'll realize that it's happening so I can get him help immediately."

My sister listened, her face showing concern and empathy as I continued to unburden myself. The words tumbled out, each admission more raw than the last. "I'm so scared I'll find him dead one morning. Or if he survives this, what his recovery will look like. Is he ever going to get back to normal, or am I destined to be more of a mother than a wife for the rest of our lives?" I paused, choking back tears before voicing my deepest fear: "Are we living on borrowed time?"

To my relief, my sister didn't judge or try to dismiss my fears. Instead, she took my hand, her grip firm and reassuring. "We're all living on borrowed time," she said softly. "That's why it's so important to cherish every moment we have together."

Her words, simple yet meaningful, pierced through the fog of my anxiety. She continued, "Losing a spouse is one of the scariest things to think about. But I know you, and I know you'd do anything for Jeff." Her eyes met mine, filled with unwavering confidence. "You need to push those dark thoughts aside and keep moving forward. Focus on helping him with his recovery."

As she spoke, a sense of relief washed over me, unraveling the knot of tension I held inside me. My sister's wisdom and support soothed my frayed nerves. For the first time since Jeff's stroke, I felt truly heard and understood. The simple act of sharing my burden had lightened it considerably.

This conversation became a turning point. While it didn't magically erase my fears or solve the challenges ahead, it gave me the strength to face them. I realized that I didn't have to navigate this journey alone. Opening up to my sister not only provided me with much-needed emotional support but also reminded me of the importance of seeking help when needed.

From that day forward, I made a conscious effort to be more open about my struggles, understanding that vulnerability had not been a weakness, but a necessary part of my healing process. My sister's support became a crucial lifeline, helping me maintain the strength and resilience I needed to continue supporting Jeff in his recovery.

She was right. Despite feeling overwhelmed, I had to keep helping Jeff with everyday tasks and relearning basic skills. Jeff was my world. I would not give up on him, but my aggravation continued to fester. Constantly having to teach him what he used to know was frustrating, and I was equally frustrated by his reactions in public after the stroke.

Chapter 6
Social Anxiety

*Nobody realizes that some people expend tremendous
energy merely to be normal.*

Albert Camus

The first time I noticed Jeff's fear of being in public was on
our way home from the hospital. He had been requesting a
thick, juicy burger and French fries. The hospital food was, in
his words, bland and gross. There was a local tavern on the way
home that had amazing burgers. I was more than happy to have
a meal that didn't consist of junk food.

When we arrived, I had to help Jeff with the stairs and opening the door. He couldn't grasp the simplest concepts of how to walk into a building. The frightened look on his face told me he wasn't comfortable in this environment.

He glanced around the place, saying, "I don't like this. I want to go."

Instinctively, I made him stay. If he was going to recover, I could not shelter him from being out in public.

We sat in a booth, far away from everyone else. He kept looking around, surveying the place and people, as if he were an anxious child wanting to escape a scary situation. Observing this was hard, considering Jeff's outgoing personality. We were sitting in a restaurant booth, as we had done hundreds of times before, and he was petrified. A part of his recovery would have to include making him more comfortable in public.

"Look at me," I said, waiting until he lifted his eyes and met my gaze. "Pretend we are the only two people here." It was the only thing I could think to say. I held his hand for reassurance.

He slumped his head and whispered, "I don't like this."

"You're going to be okay. We are just going to eat some food and go home."

I could have ordered food to go and let Jeff wait in the car, but I didn't want him out of sight. Plus, Jeff had already expressed his determination to achieve full recovery. If that was his goal, that's how we would tackle these uncomfortable situations.

The fear of public places was an unexpected effect of the stroke. I needed to witness more of his reactions in public to see how to navigate his social anxiety. His recovery needed to start immediately, so we stayed.

The waitress came to take our order. Jeff kept his head down.

My voice came out louder and more forceful than I usually speak, "We'll both have a burger with everything, fries, and Coke to drink."

"Sure. I'll be right back with your drinks," she said, side-glancing Jeff.

My duties now included telling strangers what Jeff wanted. This became even more apparent when she brought our food and asked Jeff if there was anything else she could get for him. We both waited in silence for his answer. When he didn't say anything, I found myself, for the first time, telling an outsider about our recent disaster.

"He had a stroke four days ago." This became my pattern of defending Jeff against those who stared at him with rude curiosity.

We had to explain this to people many times during his recovery. I suggested that Jeff use this approach when he encountered situations that he couldn't handle alone.

The restaurant experience showed me how Jeff's stroke had affected his confidence in public. While he wanted to maintain his independence, these social interactions posed unexpected challenges.

Jeff was determined to do things on his own. He started going to the grocery store by himself, but sometimes returned empty-handed.

"Ummm, where's the stuff you went to get?"

"I got up to that thing, that thing, you know the thing where you pay?" His anxiety was growing. "And I didn't know how to use it, so I just left the stuff there and walked out." He dropped his head in defeat.

I wrapped my arms around him. "Oh, honey, why didn't you ask for help?"

"I'm a grown-ass man who shouldn't need help paying for stuff at the grocery store. I'm so stupid."

Feeling a twinge in my heart, I had to give him a coping strategy: "First of all, you are not stupid. You had a stroke. You are still recovering. But until you are fully recovered, you have to ask for help. Just tell people that you are recovering from a stroke and ask them to help you. People won't say no to you or make you feel stupid."

People were generally kind and quick to help Jeff. He regularly used this strategy, which made him more comfortable going out and doing things independently.

Familiar settings were also a source of anxiety. Jeff had been incredibly outgoing and sociable before his stroke, but it wasn't until the second month of his recovery that he was ready to tackle a social setting. Thinking back to his behavior at the tavern, I wondered what his reaction might be. We would be amongst friends, but would that make a difference in how comfortable he felt?

Jeff cowered in a corner, away from others.

"Are you okay?" I asked.

"I don't like this," he said with a nervous glance around the room.

"Tell me what you don't like," I said. This wasn't going as well as I had hoped.

"There are too many people all talking at once. And it's too crowded."

Not only could he not keep up with one subject at a time, but he also couldn't follow multiple conversations happening simultaneously.

In less than half an hour, he asked to leave.

This pattern continued for months throughout his recovery. When Jeff was ready to leave, we left. There was no persuading him to stay, despite his friends' attempts. I was craving social interaction, but Jeff wasn't fully prepared for it. Whether we were in public or at a friend's place, if he became withdrawn, it was time to leave. This could happen after twenty minutes or four hours. I learned to anticipate what would trigger his anxiety and planned our social events accordingly.

I declined invitations to places I knew he couldn't handle, such as crowded or loud places. Anything that took place after 9 PM was not an option. He usually fell asleep between seven and eight. Jeff's stroke had significantly impacted our social life, and even simple tasks like running errands became difficult to manage.

We were at a department store. Jeff was in the men's department looking at shirts while I ran to the restroom. When I returned, he was standing in the middle of the men's department, rubbing his head with a fearful expression.

"Are you okay? What's wrong?"

"My brain shut down."

Whenever he forgot what he was doing or felt uneasy in a particular situation, he would use this phrase. According to him, "brain shut down" meant his mind went completely blank.

Apologetically, I said, "I will never leave you alone in a store again."

Shopping had become yet another inconvenience. Jeff had to be in my sight at all times, or he would become anxiety ridden. I stopped leaving him alone in public and shopped alone whenever I had the chance.

When it came to other social situations, Jeff found traveling particularly stressful. It always started at the check-in kiosk.

Repeatedly, he asked me, "Did you do it right? Did we get everything?"

Deep breath. I tried not to lose my patience.

Feeling the persistent flow of the Transportation Security Administration (TSA) line, I gently responded, "Yes, I have everything. Now, we are going to walk over to the TSA line. Put your license in your wallet. Put your phone, wallet, and anything else you have in your pockets in a bowl. Take off your belt and shoes and put them in a bin. Walk over to the TSA agent, and she'll tell you when to get in the X-ray machine."

Jeff started rubbing his head from front to back with his eyes closed. This had become my signal that he was feeling overwhelmed. Even though each instruction was said slowly, it slipped my mind that he could only understand one thing at a time. To me, going through the TSA line was one event. To Jeff, it was a series of too many tasks to handle. In rattling off what he needed to do, Jeff just heard a bunch of gibberish. He described it as Charlie Brown's teacher. Remembering this, I slowed down my instructions.

One by one, I explained each step until he completed them. If any TSA agent gave me a strange look, I told them he was recovering from a stroke. Getting through TSA became a lengthy process for us. I hoped that the more we traveled, the less anxious he would be. Jeff's comfort level with traveling seemed to be improving until we had to go through customs.

We were flying home from St. Croix. When you fly from there to the States, you must go through TSA and Customs. TSA has become a bit easier for us because we obtained the TSA PreCheck. There were still instructions I had to give Jeff, but he wasn't as anxious. However, going through Customs pushed him over the edge. We had to wait in line forever. Jeff started tapping his foot. As we approached the Customs booth, he had a panicked expression.

"It's going to be okay. Just answer the questions she asks you," I whispered. *I can always use the "he's recovering from a stroke" card if needed.*

She asked me a few questions. I answered them abruptly while keeping Jeff slightly behind me. She handed me our passports, and as I turned, she said something to him. He responded and started walking towards me. I don't know what either one of them said, but it was a relief that we weren't detained. Only when we were seated in the waiting area did I realize how the entire transaction had affected Jeff.

He broke down in tears.

It was painful seeing him so emotional. I put my arms around him and let him cry on my shoulder. When the crying slowed, I got down on my knees in front of him and told him to look me in the eyes.

"Everything is okay. I'm here with you." He was gripping my hands tightly.

54

"All we have to do now is get on the plane." The tears had stopped.

"I'm sorry this is so overwhelming for you."

He took a deep breath. "I don't want to be like this."

With half-hearted belief, I said, "It's going to get easier. The more we travel, the easier it will get." Sometimes, I wondered if I said these things because I needed to hear them.

As I watched Jeff struggle through another social interaction, the weight of our new reality settled heavily upon me. The man who once thrived in crowds, who could strike up a conversation with anyone, now cowered from the very experiences he used to love. Our world had shrunk, confined by the invisible barriers of Jeff's anxiety and my constant vigilance.

These social challenges weren't just Jeff's to bear – they had fundamentally altered our life together. Our once-vibrant social calendar now lay in tatters, each invitation a potential minefield of stress and unpredictability. I found myself mourning the loss of spontaneity, the ease with which we used to move through the world.

Yet, amid the frustration and longing for our old life, I saw glimmers of hope. Each time Jeff pushed through his discomfort, each small victory in a public setting was a testament to his resilience. We were learning to navigate this new landscape together, finding ways to adapt and persevere.

As we continued to face these social hurdles, I realized that our relationship was evolving. We were no longer just husband and wife, but partners in recovery, each of us learning to see the world through new eyes. While the path ahead seemed daunting, I held onto the belief that with patience, understanding, and love, we could find our way back to a life filled with joy and connection – even if it looked different from the one we'd left behind.

The social anxiety he felt from traveling seemed to be one of the toughest phases of his recovery. It was hard on me, too. Traveling had been one of our great loves. Being at the airport was exciting and fun. Now, it made us both anxious. Despite my anxiety, I would keep helping Jeff through our travel adventures. If he wanted to recover completely, we would continue to travel until he was comfortable.

Throughout his recovery, I kept encouraging Jeff to strive to be more comfortable in certain situations. I still made him go to stores with me. We participated in social events, even with crowds. We still traveled. He was getting more comfortable in social settings, but we still left when he wanted to go. For once, I would have liked to stay out until I was ready to leave. Unfortunately, this wasn't something I could talk to Jeff about.

Making an effort to conceal my irritation from him, I kept my negative emotions to myself. If he saw me annoyed or irritated, it upset him. Not wanting my annoyances to affect his recovery process, I made a conscious effort to avoid venting my frustrations to him.

But one day, I snapped.

Chapter 7
Patience

*Have patience. All things are difficult before they
become easy.*

SAADI

I lost my patience.

For weeks, I made a strong attempt to control my temper
and shield Jeff from my emotions. As the first month of recovery
passed, the pressure became unbearable. I reached my breaking
point, and my patience reached its limit. It was an inevitable
outcome.

Two months before his stroke, Jeff's mom passed away. We were working on cleaning out her house and settling the estate. As an only child, Jeff had to handle everything himself. We were a few months away from closing the estate when he had a stroke.

Now, I found myself dealing with the banks, the lawyer, the real estate agent, and how to dispose of unwanted items from his mom's house. I just wanted to scream! This was not supposed to be my responsibility. I was supposed to be the support team, helping Jeff on the sidelines, not managing his mom's estate.

A couple of weeks before the house closed, Jeff worried about getting everything done. Much like his behavior before his stroke, he wouldn't ask anyone for help. Early in the morning, he would be cleaning out his mom's garage, lifting heavy objects and moving things around. I constantly worried about him having another stroke and not surviving. He was doing physical labor since the day after he got home from the hospital. Against my advice, he refused to prioritize his recovery. The only way to appease Jeff was to follow his instructions.

We walked around his mom's property as he pointed out what was trash, what needed to be moved to our house, and what remained on the premises. I made a mental note of everything, and we headed to lunch.

Three times on the way to lunch, he told me his plans for all the stuff at his mom's house. THREE TIMES. On the way home, he told me TWO MORE TIMES. I couldn't take it anymore. I lost it.

My mini tirade was loud and mean. "I know what you want to do with your mom's stuff. You told me when we walked around the property. You told me three times on the way to lunch. And now, this is the second time you are telling me on the way home. You don't need to tell me again. So, could you please stop telling me? Fuck!"

His face scrunched into an exaggerated frown, and he hung his head as if being scolded. When I noticed the tears rolling down his cheeks, my heart sank. We continued home in agonizing silence.

At home, I apologized for losing my patience, "Hey, I'm sorry I yelled at you. I've been trying really hard not to lose my patience with you. It's just that you already showed me what you want to do with all of your mom's stuff. Plus, I have to call for a dumpster, make sure our realtor has everything she needs, and work with the attorney to finalize everything. It's overwhelming me, and I got frustrated and took my anger out on you."

Still with a sad look on his face, he said, "I'm sorry, I'm a six-year-old man."

"No. You are not. You are a man recovering from a stroke. And I need to be more patient with you. I'm going to try harder. But please try to understand that this is hard on me, too."

Unfortunately, I do have to treat him like a child. The whole apology resembled explaining to a child why "mommy" was mad. My angry outburst was the result of Jeff being replaced by this child-like person whom I have to explain everything to and figure out what he is trying to say. I had to teach him everything as if he were a child, learning something for the first time. It wasn't only exhausting, but also frustrating. I had no desire to treat my husband like another son.

The delicate balance between being Jeff's wife and his caregiver became an increasingly complex struggle. These dual roles often felt at odds with each other, pulling me in opposite directions and leaving me emotionally drained.

As Jeff's wife, I longed for the intimacy and partnership we once shared. I missed our playfulness, our shared dreams, and the simple joy of being equals in our relationship. There were moments when I caught a glimpse of the old Jeff—a familiar laugh, a knowing look—and my heart would swell with hope. But these moments were fleeting, quickly overshadowed by the demands of his care.

In my role as caregiver, I found myself doing things I never imagined would be part of our marriage. Teaching Jeff to brush his teeth, helping him dress, and explaining basic concepts felt more like being his mother than his spouse. The shift from partner to nurse was unsettling, and I often struggled with feelings of resentment, followed quickly by guilt for having such thoughts.

The physical aspects of our relationship had changed dramatically as well. Intimacy, once a natural and joyful part of our marriage, now felt complicated and fraught with uncertainty. How could I balance my desires as a wife with my responsibilities as a caregiver? The line between loving touch and medical assistance had become blurred, and I found myself hesitating, unsure of how to navigate this new territory.

Moreover, the emotional toll of caregiving often left me depleted, with little energy for the nurturing of our romantic relationship. The constant worry, the vigilance, the decision-making—all of it consumed me, leaving little room for the spontaneity and lightness that once characterized our marriage.

I found myself mourning the loss of our previous dynamic, even as I committed myself fully to Jeff's recovery. There were days when I longed to simply be his wife, to have a normal argument about household chores or plan a carefree weekend getaway. Instead, I was constantly toggling between roles—teacher, nurse, advocate, and somewhere in between, trying to still be a wife.

Despite these challenges, I refused to give up on the idea of maintaining our marriage amidst the caregiving. I began to seek out small ways to connect with Jeff as his wife—a lingering handhold, a shared joke, a moment of quiet understanding. I tried to carve out time, however brief, where we could just be us, without the shadow of stroke recovery looming over us.

Balancing these roles remains an ongoing struggle, a daily exercise in patience, love, and self-forgiveness. I've come to understand that there's no perfect balance, no magic formula for being both caregiver and wife. Instead, it's a delicate balancing act, constantly adjusting to Jeff's recovery and his needs of the moment. Through it all, I hold onto the hope that with time, patience, and love, we can find a new balance—one that honors both the vows we made and the new reality we face. It's going to take strength and perseverance.

People kept telling me I was strong. A warrior. A hero. I smiled and thanked them because what else could I do? But inside, those words felt hollow. A warrior? A hero? I felt more like a fraud. Like a bomb that could explode any second. The truth was, I was barely holding it together.

These well-meant compliments of being called strong, a warrior, or a hero put more pressure on me. Each time someone praised my resilience, I felt a disconnect between their perception and my internal struggle. Outwardly, I'd smile and thank them, but inwardly, my mind rebelled against these lofty titles.

A warrior? I felt more like a reluctant soldier, thrust into a battle I never asked for and wasn't sure I could win. A hero? Heroes are supposed to be brave and unwavering, but I was terrified most of the time. Strong? I felt like I was held together by nothing more than sheer will and stubbornness, ready to shatter at any moment.

Each day felt like walking on a tightrope, balancing the needs of Jeff's recovery, the demands of daily life, and my own tumultuous emotions. I was acutely aware that one misstep, one moment of weakness, could send everything tumbling down.

But perhaps the heaviest burden I carried was the guilt. Guilt for the moments of frustration, for the fleeting wishes to escape this new reality, for the times I longed for what we used to have. Guilt for not being the endlessly patient, eternally optimistic caregiver that I thought I should be. Guilt was my constant companion, whispering doubts and accusations in quiet moments.

I felt guilty for feeling overwhelmed, knowing Jeff was the one truly suffering. Guilty for resenting my new responsibilities. Guilty for mourning our old life when I should have been grateful that Jeff was alive. It was a heavy burden, one that threatened to break me apart.

Yet, even as I grappled with these feelings, a part of me recognized the strength in vulnerability. Maybe true strength wasn't about being unbreakable but about continuing on even when you feel broken. Maybe being a warrior meant fighting not just external battles, but internal ones too. Maybe being a hero was just about showing up every day, even when you're scared and uncertain.

I could handle teaching Jeff to rebuild his life. It was forgiving myself that felt impossible.

Chapter 8
Caregiver's Guilt

*I get up and pace the room, as if I can leave my guilt
behind me. But it tracks me as I walk, an ugly shadow
made by myself.*

Rosamund Lupton, Sister

The day before Jeff's stroke haunts me.

I can't let it go. I can't stop replaying it.

Looking back, the signs were there, but we didn't recognize them for what they were—Transient Ischemic Attacks (TIAs), often called "mini strokes." I later learned these mini strokes happen when blood flow to the brain is briefly blocked. They typically last only minutes and don't cause permanent damage. But they serve as both a warning of a future stroke and a chance to prevent it—a chance I would torture myself about missing.

That day, Jeff asked for four ibuprofens—unusual for him, as he rarely took pills. He complained of a severe headache and mentioned his vision was slightly blurry.

My stomach twisted. Something didn't feel right.

"Maybe we should get you checked out," I suggested, a familiar twinge in my gut telling me something was off.

"I'll be fine after I take a nap," he said, stretching out in his recliner.

I suggested seeing a doctor two more times, but he was convinced a nap would help. Each time, that nagging feeling grew stronger, but I pushed it aside. After all, it was just a headache, right?

He woke up feeling better, and we went to a festival that evening, spending time with friends and coworkers. Everything seemed normal.

Looking back now, knowing those were TIAs, knowing what happened the next day – not listening to that subtle instinct to get him checked out torments me. Not because I could have known what was coming, but because I didn't listen to that quiet voice telling me something wasn't right.

If we had gone to the hospital that Saturday, I could have saved Jeff from all the struggles, pains, and challenges. We could have taken preventive action to ensure he didn't have a stroke. Our lives would have remained normal, only modified by a new prescription routine and more frequent doctor's visits. That would have been an easy adjustment to make.

What I couldn't adjust to was the gut-wrenching guilt I felt for not pressuring him to get evaluated. Our relationship was the type where if Jeff said he wasn't going to do something, I wouldn't push back. I can remember very few times in our marriage when I insisted he do (or don't do) something. I should have been more persistent that day and prevented the major stroke that followed. Failing to act is a burden I carry every day, a constant reminder of how a single decision altered the course of our lives forever.

Jeff could have died during that nap, and it would have been my fault. Now, he is burdened with brain damage and trying to recover from a stroke. It's a guilt that clings to me—loud, relentless, and always just beneath the surface.

Along with the guilt of inaction, I was also experiencing all types of other guilt. I never expected to feel guilty about so many things as a caregiver. Guilt showed up frequently throughout Jeff's recovery. Most of the things that made me feel shitty about myself revolved around Jeff's care, my anger, and neglecting friends and family.

I began to feel overwhelmed and resentful. There was always so much to take care of in our lives, plus I was responsible for aiding and guiding Jeff through his recovery.

Chores around the house: cooking, cleaning, laundry, and trash, all became my duties. Then there were appointments, groceries, and insurance claims. And then there was Jeff himself. I had to make sure he did his daily hygiene routine: shower, deodorant, contacts, shave, teeth. He needed three meals a day. We practiced his speech therapy. The only reprieve I had from the chaos was when he fell asleep after lunch.

This should have been a time to collect my thoughts through journaling or doing something I enjoyed. Instead, for months, I sat around and ate junk food and watched TV. I was on a personal mission to finish *Suits*, 9 seasons, 130 episodes. Eighty-three hours and forty-six minutes indulging in self-pity, while Jeff slept. I needed to break out of this spiral, but I didn't know how.

Underneath it all, I was angry with him for no longer being my protector. One morning, as I was leaving to run errands, I walked into the garage and saw the door had been left open all night. Before the stroke, Jeff would check that all the doors were locked and the garage door was down every night before we went to bed. This was no longer on his radar. I now had to remember to be the one who locked us in for the night. Such a simple task, that I didn't want to do, and one that reminded me every evening of how our lives had changed.

The resentment grew. I resented Jeff for not getting back to his old self quicker.

Longing for our life to return to the way it was, I would curse Jeff in my head, "Dammit! How could you let your health get out of control? Why couldn't you take better care of yourself? Why did you have to drink so much and eat like shit?"

My silent screams served no purpose other than questioning why I couldn't accept our new situation. I should have felt blessed that Jeff survived and didn't leave me alone. But inevitably, the anger always morphed into feelings of guilt.

The gnawing feeling of not doing enough remained in the back of my mind. There was a constant whisper of, "We should be working on his speech."

Jeff's speech therapist gave us a folder of exercises for Jeff to continue with his therapy at home. Our insurance company would only pay for ten therapy sessions. It wasn't enough. In my opinion, he needed at least six months of therapy, possibly even a year. Yet here it was in my lap, another task I wasn't qualified for.

At first, I made his therapy a weekly routine, after breakfast every morning. This lasted for three weeks until Jeff began a multitude of excuses as to why he couldn't practice his speech. These would range from "I'm tired" to "I just don't feel like it." I pressured him for another week to continue, and then I gave up, too. How was I supposed to help Jeff get better if I couldn't push him to continue working towards recovery?

Jeff wasn't the only one I felt I was neglecting. I barely reached out to my sons. When I did talk to them, my mind was elsewhere, thinking about Jeff's next appointment or what the next learning experience would entail. My entire attention had to be dedicated to Jeff and his recovery, but being emotionally absent from my children ate at me. I spent hours beating myself up over not being able to balance my time between them.

I couldn't shake the feeling that I was letting my friends down, too. Every time I declined an invitation – a dinner, a gathering, a celebration – I knew I was slowly disconnecting from them. "Sorry, Jeff isn't up for it" or "We need to stay home tonight" became my standard responses. Our social circle shrank, along with the invites. Just another thing that made me feel like I wasn't doing enough for everyone.

Feeling like I was leaving everyone behind wasn't the worst of it. The heaviest guilt that consumed me was my resistance to being Jeff's caregiver. I didn't want to care for my husband. I wanted us to take care of each other, like it used to be. If I wanted things to be back to the way they used to be, did this mean I wasn't accepting the new version of Jeff? Could I love this altered Jeff with as much passion as I had in the past? Did I still love Jeff?

I searched my soul for the answers.

As these thoughts circled in my mind, I felt the familiar churn in my stomach—the kind that came with truths I didn't want to face. I was frustrated that this is what our life had come to. I was angry that the man I fell in love with was no longer present. I never fell out of love with Jeff, but my love had shifted from a passionate, goose-bump kind of love to a caring and compassionate love for my friend. However, I was tormented that I could even have such thoughts about Jeff. He needed me completely. Questioning my love for him brought with it selfish feelings of escaping.

In my daydreams, I escaped to a small beach town, wandering quiet streets lined with quaint shops and cozy restaurants. I imagined lying on the beach, eyes closed, letting the rhythm of the waves wash over me. No responsibilities. No one needing anything from me. No schedules, no therapy sessions, no medications to track. Just the freedom to follow my whims—to sleep late, to eat when I wanted, to spend hours reading or walking or doing absolutely nothing. In these fantasies, I shrugged off the weight of being needed, of being responsible, of being someone's lifeline. For a few precious moments, I could just be me again.

Of course, I would never leave Jeff. These escape fantasies didn't consume me like thoughts of his recovery did, but they surfaced occasionally, bringing fresh waves of guilt.

As I grappled with these overwhelming feelings of guilt, I began to realize that my emotional journey was far more complex than I initially understood. The burden of responsibility, the endless self-doubt, and the immense sense of loss were all woven together, forming a web of emotions I couldn't untangle. What I was experiencing wasn't just guilt – it was a form of grief. A grief that was unique and challenging because Jeff was still here, yet so much had changed. This realization led me to explore the stages of grief and how they applied to my situation as a caregiver of a stroke survivor. My journey through guilt was just one part of a larger process of grieving and, ultimately, accepting our new reality.

Chapter 9
Stages of Grief

*Grief is not a disorder, a disease, or a sign of
weakness. It is an emotional, physical, and spiritual
necessity, the price you pay for love. The only cure for
grief is to grieve.*

Earl Grollman

Grieving for someone who is still alive is called ambiguous grief or is often referred to as ambiguous loss. It involves a deep sense of loss and sadness without a death. The person you love is physically present but psychologically absent.

I grieved the loss of my husband. Even though Jeff didn't die, his stroke took him from me. The man I spent over a quarter of a century with was "gone", replaced by someone who needed help in every aspect of his life. I didn't recognize him or our relationship.

As the reality of our new circumstances settled in, we both experienced grief over the loss of his identity. Jeff had been a strong, determined, opinionated man. He was my rock, my protector. Now the roles were reversed, but I was hesitant to assume the role of the strong one in this relationship. That was Jeff's role. I feared he would never return to his former self, and our once strong and fulfilling relationship would never be the same.

Unfortunately, we had lost something that was once amazing. Before the stroke, we embraced the freedom of early retirement. Every Wednesday became our "Retirement Field Trip" day—a chance to explore somewhere new or revisit places we'd once enjoyed. One trip led us to a scenic park with dramatic rock formations and a thundering waterfall. Afterward, we found ourselves at a lakeside restaurant, eating lunch on the patio, then spontaneously stopping at a craft brewery and a local dive bar on our meandering drive home. That freedom to follow our whims, to discover new places together, to just be—it felt magical after decades of structured workdays. We were finally living the retirement we'd dreamed about.

Then Jeff's stroke hit, and those carefree adventures vanished. No more spontaneous detours or unexpected discoveries. Our newfound freedom slipped away just as we were learning to savor it.

As I reflected on our life before the stroke, I found myself moving through the stages of grief. I remembered learning about the stages of grief in psychology class. Elizabeth Kübler-Ross, a Swiss American psychiatrist, wrote about these five stages in her 1969 book "On Death and Dying." Although she discussed phases of grief following a death, I found myself experiencing these same stages after Jeff's stroke.

The stages of grief—denial, anger, depression, bargaining, and acceptance—are unique to each person. I experienced all five, though some were more intense than others.

Denial struck first. *This can't be happening to us. It's so unfair.* We had done everything right in our lives; we worked hard, raised two wonderful sons, and were genuinely good-hearted people.

I knew plenty of people with unhealthy lifestyles— overweight, alcoholics, drug addicts. None of them had suffered a stroke that destroyed their lives. Why did this happen to my husband, who was only fifty-six and had never had any major health issues?

Despite everything, it did happen. And life is not fair. As days passed, this reality became impossible to ignore, and my initial disbelief gave way to a surge of intense emotions. Denial could no longer shield me from the harsh truth, and in its place, anger began to simmer.

Not only was I angry—I was fucking pissed. The unfairness of what happened to Jeff, to me, and to us as a couple made my blood boil. My husband's brain damage had altered not just who he was, but who I was as well. Our anticipated future crumbled, replaced by a reality I never imagined for us.

What infuriated me even more was being forced back into the role of caregiver just when I thought my time for self-exploration had finally arrived. We had spent the last ten years caring for Jeff's aging parents, and I had quietly told myself that once that chapter closed, I'd finally focus on me. After years of prioritizing others' needs, I was on the cusp of pursuing my passions. Now, those dreams were postponed indefinitely. This burning anger—though understandable—was ultimately destructive, benefiting neither Jeff nor me.

Jeff was also angry. He often had rage-filled moments that erupted unpredictably. His frustration with simple tasks intensified until he'd snap, usually at me. "I don't need your help!" he'd shout, or "You don't understand!" These words stung, especially because I was trying so hard to help him. While I couldn't comprehend exactly what he was experiencing, this stroke had upended my life, too. Every time he pushed me away or lashed out, I felt the divide between us grow wider.

I tried to remain understanding, reminding myself that his anger stemmed from his struggle with his new limitations. However, maintaining my composure in the face of his fury became an increasingly difficult exercise in self-control. I found myself walking an emotional tightrope, balancing empathy for his situation with my own need for respect. As these incidents accumulated, I felt my patience wearing dangerously thin.

"Jeff, you can't keep treating me this way. I am not your personal punching bag. I am the only person here for you on a daily basis. You're making me feel like shit. Like I'm not doing enough for you. I get that you're angry this happened to you. I'm pissed about it, too. But we have to work together as a team. As the partners we have always been. You need to stop lashing out at me. I can't take it anymore." A tear trickled down my cheek.

He hung his head, "I'm sorry. I don't want to be like this."

"I know, honey. But you have to stop taking it out on me. I'm angry, too. And I'm trying to be sensitive to how you're feeling during your recovery, but I can't have you treating me this way."

These conversations were tough. They were needed on several occasions. Jeff's cognitive abilities, specifically his receptive aphasia, left me wondering if he understood me.

Then, a small glimmer of the old Jeff appeared, "I always want you to tell me when I am being an asshole to you. I love you and I don't want to be mean to you. I'm sorry."

Though anger initially served as a temporary outlet for our pain, it didn't provide solutions to our problems. As Jeff and I learned to manage our anger, I realized I needed to focus on what I could control. My rage gradually gave way to a desperate need to restore order to our chaotic lives. This transition marked my entry into the bargaining phase, where I grasped for any sense of control over our new reality.

The bargaining stage of grief brought a desperate belief that I could somehow influence Jeff's recovery through urgent begging.

As Jeff slept, I would silently plead for help, *Dear God, if you're out there and can hear me, please help Jeff get better. If you're as almighty as they say, can you fix him? If you bring him back to me, I'll try to be a more religious person.*

Or sometimes, because I still feel her soul around me, I would ask my grandmother for assistance, *Hey grandma. I need you right now. I know you never met Jeff, but he's a really good guy. You would have loved him. Can you see if there is anything you can do to help him? I promise to have a closer relationship with my mom if you can help me with this.*

I couldn't tell if my prayers were working since Jeff was still struggling daily.

80

The bargaining phase intensified as I wondered what else I could do to help him.

I found myself frequently coming up with "if/then" statements:

If I help Jeff with his aphasia, then he will talk normally again. I was constantly correcting Jeff's pronunciation of words and drilling him with speech therapy exercises.

If I get him healthier, then he won't die on me. We went on walks, and I cooked healthier meals.

If I pushed him hard enough, then we could return to some form of normalcy. I would do anything to get back to normal.

His recovery had become my sole purpose, as if I were the only one who could make him better. Intellectually, I knew he had to work on his recovery, too, but emotionally, it all rested on me. As my attempts to negotiate with fate proved unsuccessful, a heavy sadness settled over me. The realization that I couldn't change our circumstances through sheer will or effort ushered in a period of hopeless depression, not only for me, but for Jeff, too.

The first time I noticed any sign of depression was a few weeks after his stroke. Jeff sat silently in the living room, staring off into space. I sensed something was off and asked if he was alright.

"I almost died."

I inhaled sharply, "Yes, dear. You almost died that day, but you didn't."

For the first time since his stroke, he verbalized the severity of what had happened.

"Every morning, when I open my eyes, I stare at the ceiling thinking, Ok, I'm still here."

Hearing those words filled me with deep sorrow, but I responded with even stronger ones, "Jeff, you lived that day for a reason. Think of this as a second chance at life. You're going to have bad days, emotionally, but you're still with me. And as tough as your recovery may seem, you need to keep fighting through it. You've made a tremendous amount of progress already. Our lives will not be this way forever." I held him as he broke down in tears.

On his darkest days, Jeff's inner turmoil erupted in heart-wrenching declarations: *I don't want to be like this anymore. I should have died that day. I'm stupid. I'm a child. I want this all to go away. I just want to be normal again.* These raw, painful statements revealed the depth of his frustration and despair. Listening to my once vibrant, optimistic husband speak this way deflated me. The only way I knew to support him and get him out of these funks was to be positive. But being positive was so damn hard because I was frustrated about our situation, too.

Those first few months trapped me in a bubble of isolation. Our house became my entire world. I moved through our home like a ghost, going through the motions of caregiving while feeling increasingly disconnected from myself. Days blurred together in an endless cycle of caretaking tasks, each one pulling me further from the life I used to know. Even when visitors came, I felt alone—their brief presence highlighting just how isolated our lives had become. Despite feeling defeated, I couldn't bring myself to cry.

The ugly cry. The snot running down your face, guttural sounds escaping your mouth, fist clenched, punching your pillow, swollen eyes, and a belly that hurts kind of cry. It would have been an emotional purge for my soul. That's how desperately I needed to release my emotions. A child-like temper tantrum would have been a way to release the depression. Yet, it never happened.

I didn't openly cry for five months after I brought Jeff home.

My crying happened only in secret, away from Jeff's awareness. It happened in bed while he slept next to me or during long, hot showers.

I wanted Jeff to see me as strong. I didn't want to fall apart in front of him. He needed me to be his strength. Silently crying became my only outlet for the pain and emotions to briefly slip away.

It might have been easier if I had sought support from the people in my life, but I didn't lean on my friends. I didn't want to bother anyone. There was a limit to how much people were willing to listen to our struggles. They had good intentions, and I understood they cared. But when I got into the details of our daily adjustments and the emotional toll on us, their eyes drifted off. I was making them uncomfortable. So, I stopped sharing.

I preferred not to make others feel awkward. I told them, "Everything's good. Jeff's making great progress, and I'm just taking care of things around the house." This generic statement created a more comfortable atmosphere for conversation.

Yet, I felt insincere about not sharing the details of our daily lives. There was a disconnect between wanting to share my thoughts and not wanting to upset people. This proved to be a foolish decision for my mental health.

Depression grows in isolation. I was falling into that pit and needed to find a way to climb out. Relief didn't come quickly— but it began when I started to accept that our lives were forever changed. That acceptance didn't happen overnight. It came in small moments—watching Jeff laugh at a joke on TV, seeing him proudly accomplish a task in therapy, or feeling the familiar warmth of his hand in mine. These fragments of connection reminded me that while much had changed, not everything was lost.

Each tiny recognition became a stepping stone, leading me slowly from despair toward hope. I began to understand that acceptance wasn't about giving up—it was about finding new ways to connect within our circumstances. The fog of depression lingered for months, but eventually, I started to see glimmers of a different perspective. I was moving toward a place of acceptance—not defeat—but of a new, altered reality.

After months of cycling through denial, anger, depression, and useless bargaining, I reached a turning point. The realization that I didn't want to spend the rest of our lives trapped in these stages of grief hit me with startling clarity. I knew I needed to change my way of thinking – not just for my sake, but for Jeff's as well.

During one of my darkest moments, I asked myself a simple question: *Is this how you want to live?* The answer hit me hard—*No.* I was miserable, and that wasn't fair to either of us. Jeff had survived his stroke, yet I was living as if I'd lost him completely.

I realized I had a choice. I could keep grieving for our old life, or I could embrace what we had now. If Jeff was going to fully recover, he needed to know I was there for him unconditionally, not just as his caregiver, but as his wife who still loved him deeply, cognitive impairments and all.

Finally, understanding I couldn't live a life filled with constant grief, I decided to write Jeff a letter. I would express to him the love that remained in my heart and how I wanted to approach our future. This wasn't just about accepting our new reality; it was about embracing it and reaffirming our love in the face of these challenges.

Writing the letter became a cathartic process, allowing me to organize my thoughts and emotions. As the words flowed onto the page, I felt a weight lifted from my shoulders. This letter became both a promise to Jeff and a reminder to myself of the strength of our bond and the path forward I was choosing.

Through tears and a quivering voice, I read the letter to Jeff.

My Dearest Jeff,

I've realized that I've been waiting for you to come back to me. For life to be normal again. For you to get back to normal.

But that is never going to happen. You've been through a traumatic event in your life. And so have I. One can never fully recover or return to who they once were after going through such a major medical event.

Instead of forever waiting for you to return to me, I want to accept you as you are. Because you are still the same person inside. You are still the man I fell in love with. You're kind, caring, and giving. You love me with all of yourself. We still have a deep bond, and I want to nurture that instead of waiting for the old you to return to me.

We've been through tough times and major challenges in our life together, and this one is possibly the worst. But I believe if we can hold onto our strong love for each other, we can come out on the other side of this, loving each other that much more.

I don't want to wait anymore. I don't want to wait for you to be "normal".

I want to give you everything I can, and don't want to hold myself back from you because it would cause so much pain if you were to leave this world while I was still waiting for the old version of you to return to me.

I want to give you all of my love. I want to love you as you are and not wait for who I want you to be.

We both changed that day. But we both changed so much over the years, and still have managed to love each other.

I promise from this day forward that I will love you unconditionally as you are, not as the person I'm waiting for you to be.

You are my soulmate, my best friend, my loving husband.

I'm sorry I got lost in wanting our life to return to what it once was.

I am grateful you are still here with me, even if you are not the same person you used to be.

And I still love you as much as I ever have.

I hope you can get to a place where you love yourself again and remember how strong we are together.

I'm sorry it took me so long to remember this, but my promise to you is to show you every day that I love you for who you are now and forever.

Heart, Mind, and Soul,
Denise

This letter alleviated a considerable burden on my mind and heart. I didn't have to wait for Jeff to come back to me. The love we shared had always been there—I just needed to bring it back to the forefront of our lives.

Reading this letter to Jeff proved therapeutic for both of us. Our tense, stress-filled days became lighter. I was able to release emotions that were keeping us from moving forward. Jeff could let go of any doubts of my love for him. I had accepted our new life and was finally able to tap into the strength we both needed.

Chapter 10
Finding Strength

Life is tough my darling, but so are you.

Stephanie Bennett-Henry

While others saw me as strong, internally, I struggled with a sense of weakness. On the surface, I played the role of the courageous, supportive wife. I smiled, reassured, and held everything together. But inside? I was a complete mess. My carefully planned future had been wiped clean, and I had no idea if I had the strength to rebuild it.

The pressure of taking care of Jeff and holding everything together was suffocating. I doubted my ability to pick myself up, dust myself off, and get my shit together. There had to be a way to transform my internal turmoil to match my public appearance.

I confided in a friend, admitting that I didn't feel strong. He texted back: *All of your strength is with Jeff right now. You will find more. It will present itself even if you don't feel it.* His words were comforting, but I wasn't sure I believed them. Was strength something I could just find? Or worse, something I was supposed to *already* have?

The only thing keeping me from drowning was the nighttime escape I found in two close friends who lived across the country. After Jeff went to bed, I'd sit on the back deck for hours, texting them. They were my outlet, my connection to life beyond caregiving. More than that, they made me feel like myself again—someone capable, someone who hadn't completely disappeared into this new reality.

One night, their words hit differently.

You're going through your own battle. Always remember it's okay to break down, cry, feel down because it's a part of it all, and if you allow yourself to get it out, then you grow stronger! You have a lot on your shoulders but there's no doubt we know you're a fucking badass!

I read that text again before going to bed, holding onto the smallest spark of hope.

The next morning, as my mind started its usual downward spiral of worst-case scenarios, something inside me shifted. Immediately, I sat up in bed and gave myself a pep talk:

You are a strong person. You got this. When have you ever given up on a challenge? You thrive on successfully completing goals. You can do this. You also would do ANYTHING for Jeff. Don't give up on him now. You are a badass. I am a fucking badass.

For the first time in weeks, I felt a flicker of energy. But I knew sheer willpower wasn't enough. I needed a plan.

My thoughts were a tangled mess of responsibilities, fears, and unknowns. I needed clarity, a way to regain control over the chaos in my head. I needed to do a brain dump. So, I grabbed four sheets of paper and spread them across the kitchen table, writing a title on the top of each one: PERSONAL. PROFESSIONAL. FINANCES. SELF. Then, I started writing.

Appointments, travel arrangements, insurance battles, unexpected charges from rehab—those filled the PERSONAL page within minutes. My PROFESSIONAL page had reminders about my book and updates for my website. The FINANCES page was the most intimidating. Jeff had always handled our money, and I had never paid much attention. Now, I had no choice but to learn. Bank accounts, mortgage, credit cards, retirement savings—what was coming in, what was going out. Jeff could no longer explain it to me, which meant I had to figure it out alone.

Then there was the last page. SELF.

It was blank.

That familiar wave of guilt washed over me. *Of course, I'm last. Again.* But I couldn't keep doing that. If I didn't take care of myself, I wouldn't have the strength to take care of Jeff. With a shaky hand, I wrote the first thing that came to mind: Make hair appointment.

It wasn't much. But it was something.

That single choice reminded me how different life had become—how so many choices, big and small, were now mine alone.

Before the stroke, Jeff and I made decisions together. Now, every choice was mine alone. There was no time for hesitation or second-guessing. The more I made decisions, the more I realized I was capable of handling them. And if I was learning to be strong, Jeff needed to become stronger, too.

He was determined to recover, but determination wasn't enough. He needed someone to push him—to *force* him, at times—to do things on his own. That person had to be me.

When he struggled with counting money, I printed elementary school worksheets with pictures of bills and coins.

"I can't do it," he'd say, frustrated.

"Yes, you can," I'd insist firmly.

I stopped handling cash for him. If we went out, he had to pay the bill and calculate the tip. Though it embarrassed him to take extra time counting money in public, I remained adamant.

"Yes, it would be easier if I did it for you," I'd tell him, "But you have to learn this again." When he resisted, I reminded him of his strong desire to get his life back to normal.

Witnessing a simple thing like Jeff being responsible for his own money made me proud. He was persevering and making small improvements. Every small victory brought him closer to feeling normal again. And with each of *his* wins, I felt stronger, too.

Not every moment was a victory, though. Some days felt impossible—days when tears threatened and exhaustion crept in, days when I wondered how I would make it through. But I kept going, holding onto my belief in my husband's recovery.

Through practice, Jeff relearned important life skills, though some tasks were more challenging than others.

Jeff was the "activities director" of our lives. He would make all the arrangements for anywhere we wanted to go or any event we wanted to attend. His resourcefulness and organizational skills were lost from the stroke. A simple task, such as ordering concert tickets on an app, sent him into a spiral.

"I'm so dumb. I can't even order concert tickets online."

"Well, you haven't done it in a while, and I even have a hard time with some apps and websites, too," I explained to him, "Let me help you."

That sentence, *Let me help you*, set him off.

"I don't want your help. I should be able to do this by myself," he raised his voice at me in frustration.

"Fine." I walked away frustrated, too. *I was just trying to help*.

From the kitchen, I could see him vigorously rubbing his head, clearly irritated. The more agitated he became, the angrier I got.

"Just let me fucking do it!" I shouted, yanking the phone from his hand.

Seeing tears well in his eyes, as he forcefully gripped his head and stared at the ceiling, brought me back to reality.

I softened my voice, "I'm sorry I yelled at you. Please don't get so worked up. It makes me worry about you. Let me get to the part where you pick out tickets, and we'll do it together."

Apologizing to Jeff was something I did a lot. It was never my intention to yell at him. Sometimes, I just reach my boiling point. I hated how my frustration turned into anger.

I wasn't frustrated with him; I was frustrated at our situation.

Again, I felt torn between wanting to become a stronger person and not wanting to deal with any of this, not wanting to be a caregiver.

After decades of routines and responsibilities, I had dreamt of a retirement filled with possibilities. My retirement dreams extended far beyond my business plans of selling clothes online and developing a website. I wanted to explore yoga instruction, community theater, and spend afternoons discovering new places. As Jeff's recovery became my primary focus, I once again set aside personal aspirations. These dreams of creative pursuits and spontaneous adventures were now put on pause, but I knew Jeff's needs had to come before my own.

Even as I grappled with the postponement of these plans, I began to recognize a different kind of growth within myself. As I challenged Jeff to accomplish what seemed impossible to him, my own buried strength began to surface.

Yet, the strength required to be a caregiver proved complex. Despite the drastic changes in our lives, I occasionally forgot the extent of Jeff's brain damage, sometimes overwhelming him with multiple topics or asking him to complete tasks he was no longer capable of performing. In these moments, I had to draw on patience, apologize, and remind myself of his limitations, learning that my emerging strength also required gentleness and understanding.

The strength to be Jeff's caregiver didn't come from one place. It came from love, from necessity, from stubbornness, and sometimes from having no other choice.

But finding this strength wasn't enough—I needed to learn how to sustain it. As Jeff's recovery continued, I realized I had to find my own ways to cope and make it through this tough time.

Chapter 11
Learning to Cope

You gain strength, courage, and confidence by every experience in which you really stop to look fear in the face. You are able to say to yourself, 'I have lived through this horror. I can take the next thing that comes along.' You must do the thing you think you cannot do.

Eleanor Roosevelt

I have always been an avid learner. If I could have made a career out of being a professional student, I would have. I love absorbing knowledge, digging into new topics, and expanding my understanding of the world. But nothing could have prepared me for the crash course I was forced into after Jeff's stroke. This wasn't the kind of learning I had chosen—it was survival, pure and simple. And at the heart of it, I had to learn how to cope.

The first and hardest lesson was self-forgiveness.

I had to forgive myself for the moments when I lost my temper, when my patience ran out, when exhaustion whispered thoughts of giving up. I had to accept that feeling overwhelmed, angry, and even resentful didn't make me a bad person. A friend gently reminded me, *You're human. Humans have emotions— even when their husbands are recovering from a stroke.*

But the darkest thoughts—the ones that filled me with the deepest shame—were the hardest to forgive.

I was terrified of losing Jeff, but I was also terrified of the life we had now. And in my lowest moments, an unbearable thought would creep in: *If he had died that day, I wouldn't have to be his caregiver. I wouldn't have to watch him struggle, wouldn't have to shoulder the weight of his recovery.* These thoughts crushed me with guilt. I should have been grateful he was alive. I should have felt nothing but relief that we still had time together. No matter how much I tried to push those thoughts away, they existed. Eventually, I had to accept that they didn't make me a monster. They made me human.

Forgiving myself was one step. Letting myself work through my emotions was another.

For months after Jeff came home from the hospital, I didn't cry. Not once. I told myself I had to be strong for him, that breaking down wouldn't help anything. But six months into his recovery, the tears came—and they didn't stop.

I cried for everything. For the past we lost. For the future I had imagined but would never have. For the way Jeff struggled to find words, to do the things that had once been effortless. Sometimes, the simplest things made me tear up—like watching him struggle to start the dishwasher.

Even commercials became triggers. I remember one about a wife with dementia. When someone asked her husband how she was doing, he simply said, *Good days and bad days, but the love is always there.* I have no idea what they were advertising, but the words cut me to my core. I saw myself in that husband— watching someone you love change before your eyes while trying to hold onto the love that remained.

After months of keeping it all inside, my soul finally released everything I had bottled up. The grief, the fear, the exhaustion— it all poured out. I cried in the shower, cried in bed, cried when I was alone in the car. And then, one day, the tears stopped.

Not forever. I know there's an ugly cry still buried inside me, waiting for the right moment to break free. But for now, I remind myself that I'm doing the best I can. And that has to be enough.

Letting my emotions out was one thing—learning how to deal with Jeff's was another.

In the beginning, I shielded him from my feelings. I hid my tears, kept my frustrations to myself, and tried to maintain a positive atmosphere, thinking it would help his recovery. What I didn't realize was that by doing this, I was allowing him to take his frustrations out on me.

At first, I justified it. Jeff had lost so much—his ability to communicate, his independence, his sense of control over his own life. I told myself that if lashing out at me helped him cope, I could handle it. But over time, it wore me down.

He snapped at me constantly. When I tried to help him make coffee or put away laundry, he'd push me away. *"I don't need your help. I have to figure it out on my own."* He treated me like I couldn't possibly understand what he was going through, as if my efforts to help were more of a burden than an act of love.

Everything shifted when he started apologizing. That's when I realized he could see how his behavior was affecting me. And that's when I knew the coddling had to stop.

I began opening up to him—really opening up. I stopped hiding my sadness, my frustration, my exhaustion. I stopped walking on eggshells to avoid upsetting him. I was done pretending I was okay when I wasn't.

That was a pivotal moment.

For the first time since his stroke, we had real conversations again. Not just about his recovery, but about us—how we were both feeling, what we both needed. And in those conversations, I found something I hadn't realized I'd lost: a sense of normalcy.

Even though we were having conversations again, I still needed something more. I needed an outlet that was just for me. That's when I turned to writing.

From the time I was eight years old, I wanted to be a writer. I still remember the first story I ever wrote—a book about a rabbit who won the lottery. I can picture myself sitting next to my mom at Parent/Teacher conferences, dressed in my plaid uniform with my legs pressed tightly together, hands folded neatly on top of the desk. Two pigtails hung from either side of my head, tied with those elastic ball hair ties. My teacher beamed as she praised my story, calling it one of the best in the class and commenting on how smart I was for my age. A sense of immense pride washed over me. In that moment, I knew. Writing was my passion. It was how I processed the world, how I made sense of my thoughts and emotions.

So, it makes sense that when my world shattered, writing became my therapy.

Journaling has been my coping mechanism for as long as I can remember. It's where I've always sorted through my thoughts, vented my frustrations, and worked through my emotions. During Jeff's recovery, it became more essential than ever.

On those pages, I admitted things I couldn't say out loud. I wrote about the mix of emotions I carried—the love I felt for my husband and the resentment I felt for the role I had been forced into. I explored my anger, my guilt, my exhaustion. In doing so, I gained clarity.

Writing helped me understand that Jeff was still *Jeff*, just different. The person I loved was still there, even if he had changed. I couldn't undo what had happened to him, but I could control how I responded. This understanding empowered me to cope more effectively.

At some point, journaling wasn't enough. I needed something more. That's when I decided to write this book.

Writing this book has become an extension of my journaling practice, but with a deeper impact. As I've pieced together our story, I've gained new perspectives on our journey. The process of organizing my thoughts and experiences for others to read has forced me to confront emotions I had pushed aside and to recognize patterns in my behavior and thinking.

There were moments during the writing process when I had to pause, overwhelmed by the weight of reliving certain experiences. Yet each time I pushed through, I felt a sense of release and understanding. Putting our story into words helped me see how far we'd come, appreciate the strength we'd both shown, and recognize the growth that had occurred during Jeff's recovery.

Moreover, writing this book gave me a sense of purpose beyond caregiving. It allowed me to reclaim a part of my identity that I feared I'd lost. The act of creation, of turning our pain and challenges into something that might help others, proved profoundly healing. It reminded me that while I couldn't control what happened to Jeff, I could control how I responded to it and how I chose to move forward.

This writing process also helped me better understand the emotional weight I carried as a caregiver. By articulating my feelings of guilt, anger, and love, I was able to step back and examine them more clearly. That reflection led to greater self-compassion and a deeper understanding of the caregiver's journey.

Perhaps most importantly, writing this book gave me hope. It showed me that even in our darkest moments, there was potential for growth, learning, and connection. By sharing our story, I felt like I wasn't just processing my own experiences but potentially helping others who might be facing similar challenges.

Throughout this journey, I learned that coping as a caregiver involved a delicate balance between caring for Jeff and nurturing my own well-being. While my focus had primarily been on Jeff's recovery, I came to realize the importance of maintaining my own identity and pursuing personal growth. This realization led me to explore ways to express myself. I wasn't only Jeff's caregiver, but an individual with my own needs and aspirations.

Coping wasn't just about surviving. It was about learning how to move forward while holding onto myself in the process. I was still figuring out how to take care of Jeff without losing myself.

Because at the end of the day, I wasn't just Jeff's caregiver. I was still *me*.

Chapter 12
Redefining Myself

*It's ironic that when you go through a tragedy, you
appreciate more. You realize how fragile life is and that
there are so many things to still be thankful for.*

Adam Grant

Jeff's stroke deeply impacted me, but also transformed me
into a stronger, more assertive, and healthier person. Initially, I
questioned my ability to handle my own pain and adjust to our
new normal. However, as I tackled demanding situations—like
settling Jeff's mom's estate or encouraging him through

recovery—my strength grew. It became crucial for me to be strong for Jeff, myself, and our marriage. Refusing to allow our love story to end, I developed the strength I needed to summon the empowered woman who lay dormant inside of me.

This journey made me more assertive in ways I never expected. In the past, I'd kept my opinions to myself, afraid of hurting feelings or making others uncomfortable. Now, I find myself speaking up when I disagree, voicing thoughts I would have once kept to myself.

This new confidence showed itself most clearly in public. I noticed the curious looks, sometimes mixed with pity, when I assisted Jeff in sorting through menu options or calculating tips. Before his stroke, such attention would have made me self-conscious, but our new reality demanded a different approach. Whether I needed to correct him, guide him, or disagree with him in public, I did what needed to be done without worrying about others' comfort. Their opinions mattered less than getting through our daily challenges.

My newfound assertiveness extended to every area of our lives. Where Jeff and I once made all decisions together—from travel arrangements to finances—I now shouldered these responsibilities alone. Managing our medical care, handling our money, planning our future—these choices became mine to make. While I hadn't asked for this role, I grew into it out of necessity.

Among the crucial decisions I implemented was adopting a healthier lifestyle. Five months after Jeff's stroke, I quit smoking—no easy task after being a smoker for thirty-six years. Witnessing Jeff's stroke motivated me to end a bad habit that had controlled me for too long. My method involved transitioning from cigarettes to vaping and eventually cutting out nicotine entirely. It was unfortunate that I had to wait until Jeff's near-death experience to finally defeat my worst vice.

Another goal was improving our eating habits. In the chapter about guilt, I discussed feeling guilty about not making healthier food choices for us. I stifled that guilt by making better choices: limiting junk food, eating at least one salad a day, and reducing carbs. These small steps toward healthy eating made a big difference in how we felt. Jeff and I even started to lose weight. While changing our eating habits was important, I knew getting Jeff active was equally vital for our overall health.

Jeff spent four weeks after the stroke sitting in his recliner. Although I understood Jeff's need for rest during his recovery, I eventually realized that becoming more active was crucial for his progress. We began by walking on the bike trail in town, then switched to the mall when the weather turned cold. We would complete five laps around the mall, aiming for 10,000 steps each day, five days a week.

These walks became more than just exercise—they transformed into therapy sessions. As we walked, I added his speech therapy practice into our routine. It was an opportunity to ask him to recite lists for me—like naming different animals, colors, or things you find in the kitchen. These were simple questions that allowed his brain to make connections it had lost.

Over time, I noticed his conversation becoming more fluid, more natural. Gradually, Jeff began expanding on topics, speaking more in depth than he had since the stroke. These mall walks gave us a daily reminder of his progress, measured not just in steps but in words and conversations. While these walks improved Jeff's physical health and gave us time together, I realized I needed social interactions with others to maintain my emotional well-being.

As an introvert and a loner, reaching out wasn't easy for me. Jeff's stroke made me confront my self-imposed isolation. For years, Jeff had been my entire social world—my best friend, my deepest connection, my everything. Sometimes I'd tell him it probably wasn't healthy that he was my only friend, but it felt enough for me. While others maintained lifelong friendships, celebrating decades of shared memories, my friendships remained surface-level. After watching so many "forever" friends drift away, I'd developed a protective shell, convincing myself I didn't need anyone but Jeff.

Now, with our connection altered by his stroke, I found myself craving what I'd always avoided—other people's company. This internal conflict churned inside me, a constant wave of confusion. How could I, someone who cherished solitude, suddenly yearn for connection? The desire to be alone battled constantly with a new, unexpected need for companionship. Losing part of my connection with Jeff revealed a truth I'd been avoiding: maybe I did need other people in my life after all.

Naturally, the first people I turned to were my family. Though I came from a large family, we hadn't spent much time together. I began meeting my older sister once a month for coffee. Driving to our first meeting, I felt uncertain about what we would even discuss. We had been close growing up, sharing a room and secrets, but adulthood had pulled us in different directions. Our interactions had dwindled to brief chats at holiday celebrations and weddings. I had looked up to her when I was younger, but I realized I didn't really know her as an adult.

Over time, those coffee dates helped rebuild our connection. Our conversations flowed easily—memories of childhood, dreams for our businesses, shared laughter over old stories. Slowly, I let go of the habit of just thinking about reaching out without taking action. When one of my siblings crossed my mind, I picked up the phone and contacted them.

Jeff's stroke reminded me just how brief our time on earth is. It made me realize the importance of expressing my love and constant thoughts to my family before it's too late. In addition to my family members, I began reaching out to friends from a lifetime ago.

I contacted my maid of honor from my first wedding, whom I hadn't spoken to in almost thirty years. It was nerve-wracking as I was uncertain if she would be receptive to reconnecting. We met for coffee, and she was still as amazing as I remembered. There was something freeing about discussing Jeff and my situation with someone who didn't know him, someone who could listen without judgment. Yet I felt a twinge of sadness knowing that if she ever met Jeff, she wouldn't meet the man I fell in love with. Still, being with her brought a sense of comfort I didn't realize I'd been missing.

We caught up on thirty years of life—school, work, marriages, kids. She looked exactly the same, though the innocence I remembered had mellowed with the years. It's remarkable how friendships can fade in your twenties and be rekindled later in life. She showed me that I could still lean on her, and she would always be there for me. That's what true friendship is all about.

Friends became more important to me than ever. My current circle offered steady support as Jeff and I navigated our challenges. We'd also met new friends who brought unexpected comfort to our lives. While many focused solely on Jeff's condition, these people asked how *I* was doing. They recognized that I was struggling too. At social gatherings, they'd quietly watch over Jeff so I could relax and let my guard down.

I hadn't always placed much value on friendship, but these new relationships felt different. They had no preconceived ideas of who I was before the stroke, which gave me permission to be my authentic self. Around others, I had learned to maintain a certain persona—to act how they expected. But Jeff's stroke had changed me. These friends accepted that change. I could speak freely, act quirky, or show vulnerability without judgment. They accepted me as I was.

While I continued to reconnect with old friends and nurture new ones, I also realized something just as important: I needed time for *myself*.

"Me Time" became essential to my sanity. I'd always believed that healthy relationships needed three kinds of time: family time, couple time, and individual time. That last one—what I called "Me Time"—meant pursuing activities I enjoyed that Jeff might not, having space to be entirely myself. After his stroke, these moments of solitude took on new meaning. They became chances to reset, to be able to breathe without the weight of Jeff's condition suffocating me.

My "Me Time" usually lasted two to four hours—just long enough to run errands alone, try my luck at the casino, or treat myself to a pedicure. These mini getaways let me step back from our new reality, free from monitoring Jeff's every move. Even routine appointments became a little slice of heaven after a while, but getting to that point wasn't easy.

I remember my first attempt at leaving him alone. I'd scheduled a hair appointment, but found myself standing in the doorway, thinking about cancelling. How would Jeff survive without me?

I shouted to him in the living room, "I should just cancel. She'll understand."

"Just go," Jeff quickly responded with slight irritation, "I'm going to sit in my chair and probably sleep."

"Ok. Your phone is on the table right next to you. If you need me, call me. Do you know how to call someone on your phone?"

"Yes, dear. Now go before you are late."

"Ok."

I walked over to his chair, put both hands on his cheeks, and stared into his eyes, "I love you." A kiss on the lips, and I was out the door.

During the entire drive to the salon, anxiety gnawed at me. The same scratchy record was spinning in my mind: *What if he has another stroke? What if he needs help and I'm not there? What if he dies alone?* A sense of calm washed over me as I pulled into the parking lot.

For the next ninety minutes, I wouldn't have to make decisions, solve problems, or worry about anything but flipping through magazines and choosing a hair color. The buzzing of

women discussing travel, aging parents, and the latest diet
trends kept me distracted. Something so mundane in my life felt
like a mini-vacation—until I returned to my car.

I sped home, convinced I shouldn't have gone—it wasn't that
important to get my hair done. I anticipated finding Jeff dead
when I returned. A realistic scene played out in my imagination.

Shaking him. Screaming his name. Calling 911. *My
husband's dead.*

I practically stumbled into the kitchen, threw my purse on
the counter, and hurried to the living room.

"Hi, Babe. Your hair looks nice."

Whew. He's alive.

It was silly of me to think something would happen while I
was gone. Wasted worry. Finding Jeff perfectly fine upon my
return not only relieved my immediate anxiety but gave me the
confidence to venture out alone again

Over time, I learned to recognize the signs that I needed this
space. When impatience crept in, when anger simmered too
close to the surface, I knew it was time for a break. These
moments alone refreshed me, calmed me, and helped me return
as a better caregiver. It became a crucial form of self-care,
keeping me from losing my sanity. Taking this time for myself
wasn't selfish—it was necessary for both of us.

Although the recovery process was about Jeff and getting
him back to where he wanted to be, I was also in recovery. A life-

altering event had happened to me, too. I needed to take time to breathe, away from Jeff. Being a caregiver had left me feeling depleted. The way I counteracted that was to make my "me time" a non-negotiable.

Each day of caregiving taught me something new about myself. Throughout this journey, I learned that coping meant finding a new kind of balance. While Jeff worked to recover his speech and memory, I worked to recover pieces of myself. Each small step I took—reconnecting with family, nurturing new friendships, claiming time for myself—helped me remember who I was beyond being Jeff's caregiver.

I wasn't just the woman who helped her husband through stroke recovery. I was still me, with my own dreams, needs, and identity. This realization didn't make caregiving easier, but it made it easier to handle. By reclaiming parts of myself I'd set aside, I found the strength to be there for both of us.

Yet even as I grew stronger, questions about our future haunted me. Each morning brought new worries about what lay ahead.

Chapter 13
Confronting Uncertainty

*We must be willing to let go of the life we planned, so
as to have the life that is waiting for us.*

E.M. Forster

Awakening in the dark silence, I would reach across the bed
to feel for signs of life. When Jeff wasn't there, panic seized me.
Was he dead in the other room?

"Jeff?" I hesitantly called his name.

No answer.

I could hear the hum of quiet voices and see the dim glare of the television in the living room.

"Jeff?" My voice echoed through the house, a bit louder and more demanding.

"Wha, what doyouneed?"

A deep sigh of relief drained from my mouth.

"Nothing. Just wanted to say Good Morning."

Our morning routine, before the stroke, was comfortable. Jeff was always up before me. The smell of coffee and bacon drifted its way back to our room, while I slowly stretched awake.

I'd shuffle into the kitchen, still blinking away sleep, to find him standing at the stove. His back to me, spatula in hand, humming some Bon Jovi song. I'd wrap my arms around his waist, press my cheek against his back, and kiss the warm skin of his neck. "Good morning, Babe."

He'd turn just enough to catch my eye, smile lines crinkling. "There's my girl."

After filling our plates, we'd settle into our recliners—his with the worn headrest, mine with the throw blanket always draped over the top. The morning news would play in the background as we ate our breakfast, planned our day, and shared the small thoughts that had occurred overnight. I loved starting each morning that way—unhurried, together, familiar.

After Jeff's stroke, mornings became the most difficult time of my day. I was trapped in bed, consumed by worries about Jeff's recovery. As time passed and his progress seemed slower than expected, reality settled in – *he may never fully recover*. Was I capable of being a loving wife and patient caregiver for the rest of our lives?

Each morning, as I forced myself to face another day of this new reality, I found myself torn between what he needed now and the memories of everything we used to share. The past, however, had a grip on me that I wasn't quite willing to let go. I missed my husband terribly, the man he used to be. I missed laughing together, planning our future together, and the shared moments of intimacy. I wanted our old life back. These were the thoughts I had to push down deep inside to be present for Jeff, but no matter how hard I pushed against them, others seemed to arise.

Unwelcome thoughts occupied my mind about Jeff having another stroke. The possibility of losing him terrified me. For the first six weeks after his stroke, I couldn't bear to leave him alone. He slept constantly, and I'd find myself checking his breathing, my face close to his. When we went to bed at night, I'd lie on his chest, convinced that if his heart stopped, the silence would wake me. This around-the-clock worry left me exhausted, unable to truly rest.

Fear followed me through each day and worsened when he went out alone. What if his brain "stopped" in public? What if someone took advantage of his confusion? He'd already gotten lost several times when I was with him—how would he manage alone? What if he died when I wasn't there? What if he never came home?

The first time I watched him drive away, I paced anxiously, imagining disasters. *He could crash our only car, leaving me unable to reach him. His phone could die while he was lost. Someone could take advantage of his confusion with money.* If I were there, I could solve any problem instantly. However, I knew I couldn't protect him forever. If I wanted any kind of independence, I needed to learn to let him go.

Each time he returned safely, my mind relaxed a little more. My worry, though never completely gone, began to loosen its grip. I trusted his friends would look after him, and gradually accepted a simple truth: if a crisis arose, I'd handle it then. There was no point in dwelling on catastrophes that existed only in my imagination.

Releasing this burden allowed me to relax when Jeff was gone. I could write, cook, clean, and do whatever I wanted during these brief periods of freedom. Most importantly, I could let go of dark thoughts about his death. In these moments, I felt glimpses of independence again, free to work on my dreams and aspirations, even if only for a few hours at a time.

Giving Jeff independence allowed me to reclaim my own. Before realizing he could manage alone, I'd lost myself in the caregiver role, barely feeling like a wife anymore, let alone a partner. But as he rediscovered his independence, I found myself again.

In some ways, Jeff's stroke hadn't changed who I was—I remained the loving wife who would do anything for her husband. What changed was my passive acceptance of our roles. I could no longer sit back and let Jeff make all the decisions. I had to become an active participant in our lives. This meant believing in my own strength, proving to myself I could handle whatever came our way. And while I grew stronger in most areas, my mind still wandered down dark paths, imagining his death.

In our twenty-seven years together, thoughts of being a widow never crossed my mind. Jeff and I had our fairy tale ending planned: growing old together, dying of natural causes in our golden years. His stroke shattered that illusion. Now I faced a devastating possibility—becoming a widow, spending twenty or thirty years of my life alone.

Losing Jeff would mean losing more than my husband. He was my partner, best friend, and soulmate. After decades together, our souls had intertwined. We thought alike, shared the same opinions, laughed at the same silly things. Our connection ran so deep that we could anticipate each other's reactions without words. Losing my other half would mean losing part of myself.

Thinking of a future without my husband filled me with mixed feelings. The loneliness would be devastating, yet I wondered about dating again. I craved affection, the feeling of being loved. If Jeff died while we were still young, could I spend decades without intimacy? The thought of being with someone else felt like betrayal, but the prospect of lifelong solitude terrified me.

I struggled with questions about grief—what was an acceptable time to mourn? I'd observed some women jump back on the bandwagon within a month, and some die, heartbroken and lonely. Our shared memories would always be precious, but I feared they might also chain me to the past. Would I recognize when it was time to move forward? Could I ever truly move on after losing Jeff?

My mind circled endlessly around thoughts of Jeff's death and my survival. No one could replace him, yet I couldn't help wondering about life alone. How does one become whole again with such a vital piece missing? Though Jeff remained by my side, these thoughts persisted.

I remembered who I was before Jeff—a fiercely independent woman raising a three-year-old son. My career was just beginning, and I'd transformed myself physically, losing seventy-five pounds. That strength emerged when I divorced my first husband, finally taking control of my life. All decisions were mine. I steered our future instead of drifting along. Then I met Jeff, and that independence faded.

Jeff became our family's leader, overseeing major decisions while I managed our home and children. This arrangement suited us—I found contentment in my supporting role, and Jeff thrived in leadership. Though equal partners, he led our path. Losing him would mean losing not just my husband, but the very structure of my life. I would have to reclaim an independence long forgotten.

The idea of making decisions with no one to share them carried a strange mix of freedom and fear. I was already the one making choices for both of us, but at least Jeff was still here, still part of the process in some way. If I were truly on my own, every decision—from the mundane to the momentous—would rest solely with me. No more "What do you think, honey?" No more shared weight of a second opinion. My life would become entirely self-directed after decades of partnership. The loneliness of such independence hit me hard.

These thoughts of being a widow served as my way of preparing for an uncertain future. Despite trying to handle each day as it came, my mind constantly wandered about our future. We'd faced countless challenges this past year, an experience I wouldn't wish on anyone.

Chapter 14
A Year of Challenge and Growth

Marriage is meant to keep people together, not just when things are good, but particularly when they are not. That's why we take marriage vows, not wishes.

Ngina Otiende

One year ago, on a random Sunday in June, I lost my husband.

He didn't die that day, but the man I knew did.

The queasiness in my stomach churned at the thought of what I'd lost. The brain damage Jeff suffered took my best friend and partner away from me. He wasn't the same person as before the stroke. I began to wonder if he would ever return to me as the strong man he once was. I had hoped our life would be back to some kind of normalcy by now.

I would love to say that after a year, Jeff was back to his normal self. Though he'd made significant progress in his recovery, he hadn't reached the level we'd hoped for. The doctors' prognosis of full recovery in six to nine months had left us disappointed—he was still struggling.

The aphasia continued to affect him, making words hard to find and causing occasional stuttering. Frequently, he expressed his anger with statements like "I hate this" and "I don't want to be like this." I hated this, too. I craved real conversations, the ability to discuss more than one subject at a time. If only I could flip a switch in his brain to make him speak fluently again.

A year felt like an eternity for me to cautiously speak with my husband and not receive any feedback. Often, I'd drone on and on about a topic before I realized Jeff wasn't saying anything. He'd stare blankly at me, and I'd become conscious of the fact that I was having a one-sided conversation. I stopped speaking, sometimes mid-sentence, and think, *He has no idea what I'm talking about.* There was no need to continue. My voice became silent.

For someone who needed to discuss and analyze everything, this silence was devastating. My conversations existed mostly in my head—no one to hear me but myself. In this lonely place, a realization struck me: Jeff must feel equally isolated. His brain held him hostage, and he was powerless to escape.

Understanding his isolation only amplified my own frustration. The more I recognized his struggle, the more aware I became of my growing impatience. My strength had grown, but my patience wore thin. As my tolerance for his slow thoughts and speech diminished, I found myself snapping more frequently, especially in ordinary situations, such as ordering from a restaurant.

With heated frustration, I barked at him, "You know what you like, so just order something you like."

Jeff had been looking at the menu for ten minutes, and I was hangry.

He set down his menu gently, raising tear-filled eyes to mine. "You don't know how difficult this is for me."

His words hit like a gut punch. My impatience got the best of me, making him think I didn't understand his struggle.

"Although I can't know 100% what you are going through cuz it never happened to me, I have been here with you this whole time. I have seen everything you have been through, and I imagine that it's frustrating that your brain won't do what you want or won't work fast enough. I know you're frustrated. I am, too. They should never have told us you were going to recover within six to nine months."

"I thought I would be better by December," He whispered.

I counted back from the day of his stroke. *Six months, like they told us at the hospital.*

"I know, honey. I was hoping so too. But you are getting better. You've made so many improvements over the past year. You've got to think about the positives."

"How am I supposed to think about the positives when I can't understand why all of this is still happening to me?"

"Maybe you are not supposed to understand it," I suggested. "Maybe you are just supposed to let your brain heal. Maybe then, everything will come back to you. You have to quit trying to understand this and just let your brain take as much time as it needs. Trying to understand it will frustrate you, and if you're frustrated, the healing will take longer. Your brain is going to take as much time as it needs to heal."

Though Jeff shrugged off our conversation when the waitress appeared, something had shifted. We'd had a real dialogue, slow but meaningful. These moments of connection, however brief, showed progress, even if Jeff couldn't see it.

He couldn't grasp his progress because the brain fog still crept in regularly. Jeff would sit in his recliner, forcefully rubbing his face as if to erase the confusion from his mind. His agitation grew as he failed to understand why his brain wouldn't get better. I wished by twitching my nose or waving a magic wand, I could make him whole again, but reality demanded I learn to be his caregiver instead.

Caring for Jeff evolved into a delicate balance of teaching and support. I learned to approach his new way of thinking cautiously: addressing one subject at a time, never talking while he was preoccupied, and explaining things gradually. His comprehension required this step-by-step approach, though he believed he'd never regain his ability to think quickly.

Despite his self-doubt, small moments of progress were beginning to emerge. "I can only do one thing at a time" had become Jeff's mantra, but a trip to the ATM proved him wrong. For the first time, he handled the transaction without asking for help. While waiting for his money, he unconsciously tapped the dashboard to a song on the radio.

As we drove away, I said to him, "Do you realize that you were just doing two things at the same time? You were using the ATM and tapping your fingers to the music. And you didn't ask me for any help using the ATM!"

My excitement bubbled over like a proud mother watching her toddler's first steps. Jeff just grinned and shrugged, "Huh."

He couldn't see past his belief that he would never fully recover, but I saw the truth. His brain was making new connections and running on autopilot more often. Despite my frustration with his slow recovery, these moments showed me glimpses of my husband returning. These sparks of hope kept me motivated to encourage his progress.

I believe in the power of positivity. Influencing Jeff to be more positive about his recovery became my mission, though Jeff's negativity often tested my patience.

He would express his frustration by saying, "I should have just died that day." Hearing that not only made my heart ache, but it also pissed me off.

It made me wonder if I was good enough to live for.

After thinking for several days about what he said, I believed I understood what Jeff meant. He didn't wish he were dead. It was his way of saying, *We wouldn't be in this mess if I would have just died that day.* I assured him I never wished he had died. I didn't want him to have one more thing to stress about. So, I planted a seed in his mind that he truly was recovering and would continue to do so through a positive mindset.

It's so damn hard to be positive all the time. Instead of continuing to get upset when he was being negative, I started to twist what he said into a positive statement.

- *I should just shut up.* → You should not be quiet if you have something to say. Try again, slowly.
- *I'm so stupid.* → No, you're not. You have brain damage, and that's just making you process things slower. Take your time. No one is in a hurry.

- *I should have died that day.* → Well, you didn't, so do something good with your life.

What I tried to do was help Jeff not believe his negative thoughts. He had to change the way he thought about his recovery in order to move forward. I was constantly encouraging Jeff to be positive. I didn't want his recovery to be hindered by negativity.

Besides my little pep talks, there were other areas in Jeff's recovery where I had to not only act as his cheerleader but also his coach. When he couldn't say the right word or started to stutter, I would slowly tell him, in a calm voice, to slow down. Where I once jumped in to finish his sentences, I learned to be patient, to give him time to find his words. If he became stuck with what he was trying to say, I gently reminded him of what he was talking about.

Occasionally, he'd stop as he entered a room and rub his head back and forth above his ears. He couldn't remember what he was looking for. We would play twenty questions until he remembered. Sometimes, it helped; other times, his frustration escalated, and he would tell me to be quiet. But I kept reminding him—and myself—that I was just trying to help.

Looking back over the year, I realized how much strength I'd developed. Like a teacher with an unwilling student, I kept pressing forward even when progress seemed impossibly slow. I tried different techniques, hoping something would work, wanting my student—my husband—to succeed. While his comprehension improved gradually, our emotional connection was taking a little longer to reappear.

I longed to feel more like Jeff's wife rather than his caregiver. It's been difficult to find a balance. My mind had been focused on protection and precaution rather than passion and intimacy. We'd become more like roommates and buddies instead of affectionate spouses. Though we had always been friends, I cherished my status as his wife even more. The wait to return to that role felt unbearable. I quit looking into my husband's eyes. I didn't want him to see into the secrets of my soul. It felt damaged beyond repair.

Then, one day, Jeff smiled at me. It wasn't the half-emotional smile he had been giving me for months. I saw this smile in his eyes. It said, "I'm coming back to you." The way he looked at me sparked something familiar. Goosebumps flooded down my arms. I hadn't felt them in a long time. Throughout our relationship, Jeff had a certain way of looking at me that would instantly cover my body with this familiar electricity. A look that was just for me, that made me feel beautiful and desired. I loved this feeling—had missed it desperately—and here it was again, unexpected and familiar all at once.

Our relationship was regaining some passion, though not as intense as before. It didn't have to be all or nothing. Jeff was still physically present. I could wait for him to mentally and emotionally come back to me, no matter how long it took. Each small improvement, each moment he accomplished something new, brought him closer to me. Piece by piece, he was making his way back. Yet, I knew he couldn't come all the way back.

I had to accept that Jeff couldn't return to being exactly who he was before. The stroke had caused major brain damage. He had to relearn how to accomplish things he had done hundreds of times in the past and how to process information he once knew. He had to understand his emotions and learn how to feel again. Simple automatic responses required practice, and still did. Though not fully recovered, daily glimpses of his old self emerged. As his recovery continued, my role as his caregiver remained central to our lives.

He needed me to find ways to teach him the knowledge he had lost. I found techniques that would not only teach him how to accomplish tasks but also help him handle his emotional and mental challenges. We had to work out strategies for day-to-day schedules and plans for the future. Throughout this time, I learned that I was stronger than I ever thought I was. Yes, there were moments of weakness, loneliness, and depression, but I couldn't live in those places. Negative emotions paralyzed me, kept me from being the partner Jeff needed.

For over twenty-five years, I proudly called myself Jeff Hoover's wife. Our relationship wasn't perfect—we'd had moments when neither of us felt proud of the other. Despite these challenges, we always worked toward something better, growing and learning from our mistakes together. Now, more than ever, Jeff needed me by his side. I remained proud to be his wife.

Being my husband's caregiver has been an intense, emotional journey. Though I never wanted this role, I continue because I love him.

Jeff is my soulmate—my soul was always meant to be with his.

Even if I don't feel like a complete wife now, I am his wife. And as his wife, I will love him in sickness and in health.

Conclusion

*...there are always going to be forces beyond your
control that can take away everything from you
except for your ability to choose how you want to
respond to the situation.*

Mel Robbins, The Mel Robbins Podcast

Imagine having that one person in your life who makes you
feel seen and heard, taken away from you in an instant. Initially,
I spent those first few days feeling blindsided and overwhelmed,

unable to function. I walked through those days lost and devastated. The world as I knew it no longer existed.

If Jeff had any chance of recovery, I needed to wake up— even if it felt like I was living a nightmare. I had to face the fact that Jeff needed me. That was the moment I truly became his caregiver, not when he had his stroke, but when I realized he couldn't survive on his own or recover without my help.

I did what any caregiver had to do – guided him through the day and taught him elementary concepts. But this wasn't the path I envisioned for our relationship. I wasn't supposed to be taking care of my husband in our fifties.

This wasn't the life I envisioned for myself, but I didn't want to stay stuck in resentment and frustration. I needed to find a way to clear my mind in order to make my days more peaceful and manageable.

To get a better handle on things, I came up with a simple strategy: I asked myself four questions to figure out how I could be a better caregiver:

1. *What am I doing wrong and why?*

2. *How do I want to feel?*

3. *How do I want Jeff to feel?*

4. *What actions or thoughts do I need to get there?*

Reflecting on those questions helped me find clarity through the ups and downs of recovery. One of the hardest realizations was how my reactions affected Jeff.

It took almost a year to stop snapping at Jeff for doing the "little" things wrong. I began to notice how my reactions—like raising my voice or using a sarcastic tone—left him feeling hurt and disappointed. Eventually, when he found his words, he started asking, "Did I do something wrong?"

That was my wake-up call. I knew I needed to pay attention to the way I talked to him.

I had to remind myself that Jeff had the social skills of a child. Would I talk that way to a child? No. So why was I treating the man I love that way? I had to soften my approach and adjust the way I was treating my adult husband.

When I answered those four questions, it became clear:

- I snapped at Jeff because I expected him to act more like an adult and not make childish mistakes. I was taking my anger out on him because I wanted him to get back to being an adult.
- I wanted to feel like a kind and understanding caregiver, as if I were giving Jeff everything I had during his recovery.
- I wanted Jeff to feel capable and confident.
- I needed to stop reprimanding him for the small, unimportant mistakes, like pronouncing a word wrong or

putting a utensil in the wrong drawer. Those weren't worth getting upset over. They were the "little things".

I still have slip-ups now and then, but when I don't control my mouth, I make it a point to reassure Jeff that he hasn't done anything wrong. Over time and with frequent reassurance, I hope to get him to a place where he doesn't feel like he's constantly disappointing others. Even though I'm working on it, I know it's a process for both of us. While I'm learning to communicate better, Jeff is still navigating his own recovery.

Two years after his stroke, he still struggles with understanding why it happened and why it's taking so long to get back to who he was. He doesn't always see how far he's come, but one of his greatest achievements is that we can now have discussions. I'm grateful to be able to have a conversation with my husband, again – even if it's slow and I do most of the talking. I knew I needed to talk to him about his anger. I lived through that stage for a long time and felt that I could get him through it.

On more than one occasion, I've told him, "You have to accept who you are now. I spent too much time wishing things were different—wishing you would return to who you used to be. But we both have to face the reality that you're never going to be the same. I'm not saying this to upset you. I just want you to know that I've gone through my own anger phase. The only way I got through it was to accept that you're a different person now.

I've come to terms with it, and I'm no longer searching for the *old you*. You need to do the same, or you'll always be angry. Do you want to spend the rest of your life angry, or do you want to find happiness in the life we have now?"

Jeff has always been someone who needs time to process the advice he is given. Often, I repeat some form of this speech to him, hoping one day it will sink in. I know in my heart he will choose to be happy.

I believe happiness is a choice, and I've chosen it for myself. In the same way, I chose to find purpose and healing through writing.

Writing this book wasn't just about sharing our story; it was about processing the journey and discovering how far we've come. Putting these words on paper helped me see our progress from a new perspective. It made me appreciate the progress we've made and reminded me why I keep pushing forward.

As I thought about our story, I realized that finding purpose beyond caregiving was essential. Balancing caregiving and self-care wasn't easy. In the beginning, I felt like I needed to spend every moment with Jeff because I feared our time together was limited. Eventually, I realized that for both of our sakes, I needed to make space for my own growth and goals. Finishing this book was part of that journey—a way to find purpose beyond caregiving.

Writing this memoir became my way of surviving my husband's stroke. I could have kept my innermost thoughts buried in my journal, but something pushed me to share. I hope that by telling my story, other caregivers will feel less alone and more empowered to navigate their own challenges.

If you're reading this and feeling overwhelmed or lost, I want you to know that it's okay. You're not alone. It's natural to doubt your strength and wonder how you'll keep going. I've been there, too. There were days when I doubted my ability to keep moving forward, but I learned that it's possible to find a way through— even when it seems impossible.

It took time to get to this place, and the process was exhausting, but it was worth it. Jeff and I have had to rebuild our lives, shaped by his challenges and our changing roles. We're still figuring things out, but we're making it work. Though our relationship has changed, it has also grown stronger in unexpected ways. We've had to rebuild, not just as individuals, but as a couple—learning to love differently while holding onto the core of who we are together.

As we move forward, I hold onto hope that our new normal will keep evolving. I no longer wish for our past life, but I dream of finding joy in the life we're building now. I'm not sure what the future holds, but I know we'll face it together—adapting, growing, and continuing to love each other in new ways.

Your journey may be filled with fear, frustration, and doubt—just as mine was. It's okay to feel like you want to give up. That doesn't make you a bad person. It makes you an overwhelmed wife trying to do what's best for her husband and her marriage. Feeling overwhelmed is natural, no matter what challenges you're facing.

Your husband's condition may be different from Jeff's—perhaps more severe, or with different challenges depending on which part of the brain the stroke affected. Every recovery journey is unique, but the strategies I've shared in this book aren't limited to one set of circumstances. My hope is that you can adapt these tools to help navigate your challenges, no matter what they may be.

Most importantly, remember to take care of yourself, too. Finding time for self-care isn't selfish—it's essential. You need your "me time", whatever that may look like for you. I learned that I can't support Jeff if I'm completely worn out. Taking moments for myself, pursuing my interests, and finding balance have made me a better caregiver and a more complete version of myself.

As a caregiver, you have to make a choice: Do you want to stay stuck in anger and grief, or do you want to find a way to move forward and love the new version of the man you married? For me, love won out. I chose to embrace the changes, accept the challenges, and continue loving my husband. You can make that choice, too.

To every caregiver reading this: You're doing enough. You're doing your best. Even on the days when it doesn't feel like it or you feel like running away, know that your love and effort make a difference. Hold on to that.

You've got this.

Stay strong. You will survive.

Denise Hoover is a writer who believes in telling the truth—even when it's uncomfortable, emotional, or messy. Her work is dedicated to midlife women navigating unexpected changes, caregiving roles, and the search for meaning when life doesn't go as planned.

In *Surviving My Husband's Stroke*, Denise opens up about her personal experience as a wife-turned-caregiver, offering not just a story, but a sense of connection and understanding to those walking similar paths.

Denise writes to remind women that they're not alone—and that even in life's hardest moments, there's still space to grow, reflect, and find strength in our stories.

DeniseHoover.com

Surviving My Husband's Stroke Companion Workbook

Are you a caregiver looking for support as you navigate life after your husband's stroke?

This workbook was created for wives who feel overwhelmed, emotionally drained, or unsure of what to do next. Prompts to process emotions and redefine your role

- Practical advice for supporting your husband's recovery
- Weekly and monthly planning pages
- Tips to organize your time, space, and thoughts
- Encouragement to help you stay grounded and organized—without losing yourself in the process

One page, one task, one day at a time—this workbook is here to help.

Learn more at DeniseHoover.com

Coming Soon ...

Midlife Choices

Are you a midlife woman feeling stuck in a rut, longing to rediscover your passions and unlock your full potential?

Filled with inspiring stories, practical guidance, and empowering exercises, this book will help you:

- Uncover your authentic desires and dreams
- Overcome limiting beliefs holding you back
- Develop a clear vision for your "second act"
- Take strategic action to turn your vision into reality

Whether you're seeking a career change, a new hobby, or simply a renewed sense of purpose, *Midlife Choices* will empower you to embrace the possibilities of this pivotal time in your life.

Rediscover your passion, reclaim your potential, and step into the thrilling unknown - the choice is yours.

Get updates at DeniseHoover.com